BY ROGER L. SIMON

Books

HEIR

THE MAMA TASS MANIFESTO

THE BIG FIX

WILD TURKEY

PEKING DUCK

CALIFORNIA ROLL

THE STRAIGHT MAN

RAISING THE DEAD

THE LOST COAST

DIRECTOR'S CUT

BLACKLISTING MYSELF

Screenplays

THE BIG FIX

BUSTIN' LOOSE (story by Richard Pryor)

MY MAN ADAM

ENEMIES, A LOVE STORY (with Paul Mazursky)

SCENES FROM A MALL (with Paul Mazursky)

PRAGUE DUET (with Sheryl Longin)

BLACKLISTING **MYSELF**

Memoir of
a Hollywood
Apostate
in the Age
of Terror

by
Roger L. Simon

ENCOUNTER BOOKS
New York   London

First edition published in 2008 by Encounter Books,
an activity of Encounter for Culture and Education, Inc.,
a nonprofit, tax exempt corporation.
Encounter Books website address: www.encounterbooks.com

Manufactured in the United States and printed on
acid-free paper. The paper used in this publication meets
the minimum requirements of ANSI/NISO z39.48–1992
(R 1997) (*Permanence of Paper*).

FIRST EDITION

LIBRARY OF CONGRESS CATALOGING-IN-PUBLICATION DATA
Simon, Roger Lichtenberg.
Blacklisting myself : memoir of a hollywood apostate in the age of terror
/ by Roger L. Simon.
p. cm.
ISBN-13: 978-1-59403-247-9 (hardcover : alk. paper)
ISBN-10: 1-59403-247-5 (hardcover : alk. paper)
1. Simon, Roger Lichtenberg. 2. Screenwriters—California—
Los Angeles—Biography. 3. Authors, American—Biography.
4. Dissenters—United States—Biography. 5. New Left—United States—
Case studies. 6. Conservatism—United States—Case studies.
7. Blacklisting of authors—California—Los Angeles.
8. Hollywood (Los Angeles, Calif.)—Social life and customs—
20th century. 9. Los Angeles (Calif.)—Social life and customs—20th
century. 10. Mass media—Political aspects—United States. I. Title.
CT275.S52136A3 2009
973.91092—dc22
[B]
2008050071

for Madeleine

TABLE OF CONTENTS

1 "ONLY VICTIMS"

I live in the Hollywood Hills in a Spanish house once occupied by Joe DiMaggio and Marilyn Monroe. Built in 1929—for Los Angeles, the early Paleolithic Age—it is not as grand as its legendary past suggests, but it does have a nice canyon view and some beautiful old Mexican tile. I bought the house in 1989, at the height of my movie career, not because of the Joe and Marilyn connection, but because I liked the place. It projected the right image for my lifestyle: a child of the Sixties turned upper bohemian lord of the Hollywood Left.

That was then. I'm not sure that person even exists any longer. I still like the house, but I no longer have that image. Indeed, I've shifted positions to such an extent that I often think I've undergone the ideological equivalent of a sex change operation.

Hence this book, which is an attempt to find out what happened—to discover how the idealistic young man who came to Hollywood fresh off the civil rights movement; created the hippie detective Moses Wine; trafficked with Abbie Hoffman, the Black Panthers, Tim Leary, and the SLA; was recruited by the KGB, and wrote (or didn't) screenplays for such paragons of the Hollywood Left as Woody Allen, Paul Mazursky, Warren Beatty and Barbra Streisand, ended up voting for George W. Bush and being publicly reviled as a neocon. How did that man come to be favorably profiled by both *Mother Jones* and *National Review* in a single lifetime? (Talk about sex change operations.)

I hope to understand it better by writing this memoir, a memoir I am typing in the very room Joe and Marilyn shared during their brief marriage. That marriage ended after only 274 days when Monroe filed for divorce for "mental cruelty" in 1954, at the height of the Hollywood blacklist.

Ironically, it was that famous list that cast an ambiguous shadow over

1

my arrival in Los Angeles back in the late Sixties. In a sense, I was a wannabe blacklisted screenwriter myself—a young man with left-wing political street cred, but without sufficient funds to live the upper middle class lifestyle of my parents. I was radical chic from the start, or aspiring to be. But it was hard to be chic in my first LA residence, a Nathanael Westian motel-ish affair on Franklin known as the "Coral Palms." Now ploughed under to make way for a mall, it was a far cry from the "Marilyn House" and composed of a dozen or so dingy, shag-carpeted one-bedrooms surrounding a cracked concrete patio and a tiny over-chlorinated pool. I lived there with my then-wife and former Yale Drama classmate Dyanne Asimow and soon our infant son Raphael. Our immediate neighbors were an unemployed actor and his Playboy bunny girlfriend on one side, and, on the other, Jill Bogart, Humphrey's seventy-year-old alcoholic sister.

I would sit by that pool, reading Fitzgerald's *Pat Hobby Stories* and Schulberg's *What Makes Sammy Run?*—the latter with its vivid portrayal of the Hollywood Left during the birth of the screenwriter's union—wondering where I fit in all this. While at Yale, I had been an anti-war demonstrator and civil rights worker. Soon enough, I was a member of the very Writers Guild described by Schulberg, an organization still operating under the ghost of the blacklist in those days. I eagerly got to know some of the formerly blacklisted writers; they were especially welcoming to me when I first joined, making sure I was invited to the necessary events—fundraisers and socials in old union meeting halls in East LA, more Workman's Circle than show biz. My left-wing reputation had preceded me.

This romance with the blacklist was cemented when, as a debutante Guild member, I went to the WGA's annual awards banquet in 1970. Indeed, I was so new that I went without realizing that this ceremony was for the most part disdained by the membership and attended only by nominees and a few Guild officers. As luck would have it, this particular awards ceremony was one of the most interesting such evenings, before or since. It has found a place in film lore because it was there that Dalton Trumbo, the most renowned of the Hollywood Ten, delivered his famous speech of blacklist-era reconciliation, "Only Victims."

Seated at a back table with my wife Dyanne and our friends the husband-and-wife screenwriter team Gloria Katz and Willard Huyck, I was excited by the drama of the occasion, but increasingly disappointed by the speech. Why was the author of *Johnny Got His Gun*, of all people, preaching forgiveness for the horrid censorship and McCarthyist blackballing of writers by the right wing? Of course, Trumbo had seen those events up close and personal. I knew them only from books and documentaries, or from those few fleeting moments when, as a six year old, I glimpsed "Tailgunner Joe" on my parents' four-inch black and white Dumont television, during the Army-McCarthy Hearings. My parents despised him and therefore so did I.

I can remember arguing with the Huycks that night, staking out, as I so frequently did, my position to the left of what I considered the weak-willed Hollywood mainstream. I relished my image as an actual Sixties activist, a reputation my agents used to my advantage, and could not so easily forgive as one of the blacklist principals himself. In fact, after that day, many of his blacklist peers criticized Trumbo and deemed him a sellout. I also felt let down by Trumbo, and judged him an old man desperate to get his career back—nothing the hardcore leftist blacklistees, such as ex-longshoreman Alvah Bessie. Of course, Bessie never had much of a career in the first place, and I didn't want to be like *him*. So I was caught in a bit of a quandary. I wanted to be like Trumbo, but a Trumbo who had kept the faith.

I doubted that my friends the Huycks would keep any kind of political faith, and they probably knew it. Willard's father had been a *Republican* state representative, of all things, and Gloria's Beverly Hills parentage was de facto suspect, unlike my Scarsdale, New York background. I assumed they were in it—the movie business—for the "main chance" and lacked the requisite ideological purity of the era. Needless to say, all of us were as ambitious as could be, regardless of our political beliefs. When Gloria and Willard achieved enormous Hollywood success only a few years later, writing the screenplay of *American Graffiti* and the bar scene from *Star Wars*—not only reaching "A-list" status but also making themselves financially independent for life while still in their twenties—I wasn't the only one who was wildly envious of them.

On the night of the "Only Victims" speech, however, I was the one whose career was in ascendancy. My first novel, *Heir*, had just been made into a film called *Jennifer on My Mind*, with a screenplay by Erich Segal of *Love Story* fame. The movie stank and only remotely resembled my book, but the novel—inspired by the true story of a wealthy Dartmouth College classmate of mine who accidentally overdosed his girlfriend with heroin—had opened a lot of doors for me, including the chance to work for Charles K. Feldman. I was the last screenwriter hired by the famous agent-producer, who had been involved with *The Seven Year Itch* (this was long before I came to live in the Marilyn House or even dreamed of such a thing), not to mention the likes of William Faulkner, Tennessee Williams, and Elia Kazan. I sat in his living room surrounded by Bonnards and Modiglianis, watching his then-wife Capucine walk in and out while he fielded phone calls from Billy Wilder, and I couldn't help wondering what the hell I was doing there. Frankly, not much. Unbeknownst to me, the man was dying of cancer, and I suspect I was really there to help him fill his time, pretending he would produce yet one more movie—a film version of Calder Willingham's *Eternal Fire*.

I worked on the screenplay in Feldman's Beverly Hills office at a mahogany desk, beneath a Degas I can only assume was real. Once a week I'd drive up Coldwater Canyon to his home when, depending on the hour, tea or cognac would be served by the staff. The aging producer, an elegant man with silver hair and tailored shirts, would put his feet up on a divan and dial Warren Beatty, telling the young actor that he had a script in the works that would be perfect for Warren and "his girl," then Julie Christie. I would come to know Beatty later in a rather different, more politically fraught way. But at that point I was peripherally involved in the glamorous atmosphere of the Old Hollywood that was even then fading fast. I was lucky to have seen it.

Feldman was, as they almost all were in those days, a liberal of sorts, and he was fascinated by me, a live specimen of the New Left. It wasn't that he expected me to breathe fire or throw bombs or anything—but he found it amusing that I planned on using the money from the Willingham adaptation to go to Stockholm, hang out with Vietnam deserters (we were in the midst of the war), and write a novel about them. I could tell that he was skeptical of my will to resist the blandishments of Hollywood and to follow through with this plan. He held out all manner of possibilities to me, including directing films before I was twenty-five. The truth is I have no idea what I would have done, but Feldman's pancreas got the better of him and my gravy train was derailed. For the moment, my options were closed. Dyanne and I and our six-month-old son Raphael were on our way to Europe.

This was the spring of that epochal year, 1968, and I traipsed around the rainy Gamla Stan—Stockholm's Greenwich Village—trying to get the inside story on the deserters. Finding them was relatively easy, but they proved to be a dull and predictable lot, lost in more sophisticated Europe and finally more interested in scoring the next joint than in discussing revolution, or much of anything else. I was unsure what to write about them.

Nevertheless, I continued across Europe with my young family, arriving in Paris days after May '68 *événements* to see the cobblestones of the Left Bank streets torn up and the buildings papered with anti-de Gaulle posters. Something was happening. My generation was about to change the world, and I wanted to be part of it. The feeling intensified when we reached London and I watched the Chicago Democratic National Convention on the BBC. Everything exciting seemed to be taking place in the American streets and I was stuck in a grungy one-bedroom over a Tube station in Belsize Park. I wanted to go home. I wanted to participate.

But I had to write my book, not least because I'd already leased a "writers' villa in Southern Spain" from an ad in *The Saturday Review*. Its owner, ironically, was the editor of London's *New Left Review*; he justified having property in Franco's Spain by saying that it allowed him to bring banned subversive books into a fascist state. Rationalization or not, he was right. The office I worked in until the spring of 1969—a separate one-room writer's house outside of a villa in the picturesque village of Mijas, Spain—was lined top to bottom with the works of Marx, Gramsci, Che Guevara, et al., a more complete library of the Left than I can recall seeing before or since in a private home. The office's picture window had a panoramic view of the Mediterranean, with Gibraltar in the distance.

Not that the fabulous digs helped me write. I spent most days poring over the *International Herald Tribune* for news of the political battles back home. Toward the end of our lease I had all but given up on working and would sit at my desk, gazing catatonically through the picture window with all kinds of gloomy fantasies going through my head, including Dyanne having an affair, *à la* D. H. Lawrence, with Esteban, the villa's gardener. Also, I was pretty much broke, my generous Charles K. Feldman "annuity" reduced to a couple of thousand bucks. I was relieved when it came time to go home.

Once back in LA, I did what any normal American boy with no prospects and no money would—I took the last of my cash and bought a house. That home, which belonged to some nice socialist friends of Dyanne's similarly nice socialist parents, was in Echo Park, a barrio plagued by Chicano gangs. I loved it, especially for the apprehensive faces of my Hollywood contacts when I told them where I lived after inviting them to dinner. But, despite the gang graffiti on the garage door, the house itself was quite welcoming, a slightly long-in-the-tooth craftsman left over from the long gone days (1920s) when that neighborhood was tonier.

It was there, shortly after returning from Europe, that I entertained *Love Story* author and screenwriter Erich Segal. Just in the nick of time, the film adaptation of *Heir* was heating up and our mutual agent, Ron Mardigian of William Morris, brought Segal over. Segal was only a couple years older than I, but vastly more famous. "I wrote a book on Plautus," were the first words out of his mouth. Evidently he wanted to make sure that I regarded him not as a mere author of schlocky bestsellers, but as a full-fledged Harvard classicist. His study of the Roman playwright, I was informed immediately thereafter—and, needless to say, without asking—had received "excellent reviews from the scholarly press." I stopped myself from giggling. Much as I instantly knew the pompous Segal was an absurd choice to adapt my "noir-ish" novel of a rich boy driving his dead girlfriend around in the trunk of his car, I didn't want to jeopardize the movie. I was still living more or less hand-to-mouth and would receive a significant check only upon filming.

In fact, I had been typing my next book practically from the moment I stepped off the boat from Europe, working against the clock to preserve my dream of becoming a writer from the encroaching reality of supporting a family. I gave up on the deserters, reaching for my subject into the world of my friends and acquaintances—the adventures of Barbara Garson and her husband Marvin. Politically speaking, they interested me more than the deserters. Barbara, a left-wing activist who had been in Dyanne and my screenwriting class at Yale, was notorious then for writing the anti-Vietnam War hit *MacBird*, a satiric Shakespeare knockoff in which a dolt-like LBJ was presented as a modern Macbeth. It ran Off-Broadway for several years. Marvin had been a somewhat less prominent Berkeley student protest figure. The theme of my book was to be what happens when a "revolutionary couple" sets out to change the world and ends up making a million in the process.

To demonstrate my growing support for women's lib, or perhaps for the shock value of a man doing such a thing, I wrote the book in the female first person, looking backwards from Barbara's point of view, or rather from the vantage of the fictional Barbara, Tanya "Mama Tass" Gesner. It was called *The Mama Tass Manifesto* and had the opening sentence, "If Emma Goldman could see me now, the only female gas station attendant in Brixton, Oklahoma." The title was printed in the curvy font of a Grateful Dead poster and the flap copy included a quotation from Chairman Mao about the necessity of picking up the gun. (It was 1970!) Instead of the normal author photo on the back, the book had a reproduction of my driver's license with the address crossed out, to give the impression of a mug shot.

Some of these packaging ideas came from my editor from *Heir*, Alan Rinzler, who bought the book for Holt, Rinehart & Winston when the manuscript was half finished. To this day, I thank him for it. It wouldn't be the last time that he'd rescue me in a moment of need, although he would never publish the book you are reading or probably anything else I write for the foreseeable future. Alan—who published seminal works like Claude Brown's *Manchild in the Promised Land* and Hunter S. Thompson's *Fear and Loathing in Las Vegas*—now considers me an apostate and recently emailed me "I knew you when...."

And he isn't the only one. At a cocktail party a few months back, I ran into the liberal humorist Harry Shearer of *This is Spinal Tap* and now of the Huffington Post. A mutual acquaintance, not realizing we had known each other for over thirty years, attempted to introduce us by asking Harry if he knew me. He replied cuttingly, "I knew Roger when he was another person." There are plenty of others who just turned away.

But am I "another person"? I will leave that to the reader to decide.

In any case, *The Mama Tass Manifesto* is steeped in the radical politics of its time, which were all around me. Echo Park had become a haven for the refugees of the Berkeley Free Speech Movement. Most of them were grouped around an organization called the Echo Park Food Conspiracy, led by the lawyer Art Goldberg and his sister Jackie, both of them 'red diaper babies' and self-proclaimed Maoist revolutionaries. Art still practices law in that neighborhood. Jackie is currently a California State Assemblywoman in the forefront of the gay marriage movement.

In those days, Jackie, occasionally accompanied by longtime California Communist Party leader Dorothy Healey, taught a course in American labor history one night a week at our house. Art, more of a glad-handing sort, ran the Food Conspiracy. The idea was to use cheap, cooperatively bought food as an organizing device, setting up a neighborhood market where young activists could radicalize the mostly Latino poor of the community. I remember the jovial Art walking among the various shoppers, thrusting his fist in the air and clapping some on the back. "Venceremos, amigos," he'd say, "La lucha continua!" The struggle continues! He interspersed his barely serviceable Spanish with smiling nods to local Asians, whose native languages he couldn't identify, let alone speak. Whenever he saw me, he'd pull me aside and say, "Hey, Roger, the struggle continues! Howzit goin' in Hollywood, man? When're we gonna get some of your movie star friends down here? Teach them a little Marxism-Leninism-Mao Tsetung thought?" It was hard to tell if he was joking or not.

But in truth there *were* developing connections between the film world and the young radicals of the time, and I was a part of them. One of my first studio screenplay assignments after returning from Spain was an original idea of mine called *The Black Wizard of the Dakotas*. Inspired by John Ford and the left-wing Brazilian filmmaker Glauber Rocha— and based on information I'd gleaned from Jackie's labor history class— *Black Wizard* was a Marxist Western (with a hint of magic) about the nineteenth-century Colorado mining strikes. The script was developed at Warner Brothers for director Paul Williams. Williams had just made a critically-acclaimed but low-budget film called *The Revolutionary*, the tale of a college student known as "A" (played by Jon Voight, today one of the few movie star supporters of the Iraq War) who rebels against his bourgeois father and gets caught painting anti-capitalist manifestos on the wall. But I don't think even Williams and his producer partner Ed Pressman had any idea of just how left my script would be. (Let's say Maxim Gorky couldn't have done better.)

Not that the executives at Warners seemed to care. There was no mention of the script's politics in our meetings, but they eventually chose to make another film with Paul Williams on a subject they deemed more commercial: marijuana. Unfortunately, *Dealing: Or the Berkeley-to-Boston Forty-Brick Lost Bag Blues* was a flop. Williams—whose career skidded and who has had trouble making movies ever since—went on to attempt to help fugitive Black Panther Huey Newton escape to Cuba under bizarre and ironic circumstances, which I witnessed.

That Panther connection may have been what attracted Pressman and Williams to me in the first place. They probably knew something about it when they came to dinner in Echo Park the first time. At the time, I donated some of my Hollywood money to the Black Panther Breakfast Program; I regarded this humorously as a tithe, though it was considerably less than ten percent. (The Breakfast Program, which fed inner city children, was well publicized then and helped distract from some of the Panthers' more controversial activities, like drug dealing and murder.) Around ten o'clock at night and often unannounced, some of the brethren in black berets and leather jackets would arrive at my house with a half-dozen or so kids in tow. "Hey, Rajah," the ringleader would say, "these children got nowhere to go for ham 'n eggs tomorrow." He knew how to con a Hollywood mark when he saw one. How could I turn them down? I would write a check for a couple of hundred bucks—payable to cash, of course—trying not to wonder whether the money would be used for food or for AK-47s. I guess I didn't care to know, so long as they left quickly. I have to admit I was a little nervous having the Panthers in my home. I was always pacifist by temperament, even when I flirted with more violent types, and I did have children of my own in the house, first Raphael and then Jesse, born two days after Christmas 1970.

I don't remember the names of the Panthers who came those nights— they were foot soldiers—but I did meet some of the leadership then, including Eldridge Cleaver, his wife Kathleen, and Elaine Brown, their Minister of Information, who played first-rate blues piano at fundraisers. Brilliant and sexy with a bourgeois background, Elaine was the kind of woman that fed the fantasies of young liberal Jewish boys from New York until they broke into night sweats. Just knowing the Panthers then was a great talking point in Hollywood meetings. Of course, I didn't know them *very well*, but who cared and who knew? The point was to give off a whiff of radical danger, but not so much that people would be worried about working with you.

The radical edge was closer then. Granted, most young movie people dabbled in this kind of activity for show, or to be part of a particular crowd, but there were those hardcore types who abandoned the film industry to become actual members of the working class. I knew some recent graduates of UCLA Film School who'd quit the movie business to join the various industrial assembly lines—not to say that their film careers were all that promising in the first place. Nevertheless, they went about the business of being "de-classed"—just as people had in the Thirties, although these were the early Seventies and Stalin was already long dead, long exposed as a tyrant of epic proportions. One man—an aspiring director named Peter Belsito who had written a script called "Stalin's Children"—and his wife Judy moved from their groovy cottage on the Marina Peninsula in Venice to grimmer digs in City Terrace, in the heart of Latino East Los Angeles. Peter joined the line at the Buick plant in Southgate; Judy, who had a degree in chemistry from the University of Wisconsin, got a job as an information operator with the telephone company so she could organize workers there.

A group called the California Communist League, led by a man named Nelson Peery, was at the center of this extreme left-wing organizing. And when I say "extreme," I mean it. At the invitation of the Belsitos, Dyanne and I attended a barbecue in East LA given to introduce members of the entertainment industry to the CCL, presumably to enlist us. The problem was, although there were well over a hundred people there, the only actual *working* movie person, besides Dyanne and me, was our friend Linzee Klingman, who later went on to edit *One Flew Over the Cuckoo's Nest*. And she had come with *us*. We tried to make the best of an awkward situation, munching on the tamales while perusing a long table of pamphlets—all of them produced by the Labor Party of Albania and most authored by its chairman, Enver Hoxha. Albania was evidently the only socialist country pure enough for the California Communist League. Even Mao's China, still in the midst of the Cultural Revolution, was suspect.

After lunch, Nelson addressed the attendees. He warned us, particularly we three film people, that the revolution was nigh and that we had to decide which side we were on because afterwards there would be an accounting. If we stood with the revolution, we would be rewarded. Otherwise, there was no telling what would happen. He frowned ominously.

I remember dismissing this as pure insanity, then wondering: *What if he's right?* I didn't want to end up in a reeducation camp—or worse. Absurd as it sounds now, I felt then that it was best to keep my options open. Even if Nelson was an ideologue, who wouldn't sympathize with the working-class blacks and Latinos who populated the barbecue that day? They were a lot friendlier than the rich Hollywood types I worked with, far less competitive and slower to judge. If there was going to be a revolution, I wanted to be on their side. And maybe, despite all evidence, something *was* about to happen. The "illegal" war in Asia was still raging. The inner cities were in turmoil. When people asked me my ambition in those days, I said, only half in jest, "I want to be Minister of Culture." I even thought of having those words on the frame around my license plate, the way some had "My Other Car is a Porsche."

Actually, my car was a Mercedes, a used or (in modern parlance) "pre-owned" one I'd bought from the Republican father of Willard Huyck, the screenwriter with whom I'd shared a table the night Dalton Trumbo spoke. I'd driven the Mercedes to that Writers Guild event, which was at the Beverly Hilton, but not to the barbecue in East LA. For that occasion I'd preferred our more anonymous Volvo, by then fairly beaten up and victimized by a particularly hideous $29.95 magenta Earl Scheib paint job.

My life was filled with this kind of schizophrenic behavior, and would be for years to come. My inability to reconcile my beliefs and my lifestyle probably had something to do with my anger at Dalton Trumbo that evening. Speeches about reconciliation didn't fit with my self-image—not as a "revolutionary" or as an aspiring Hollywood "player." I wanted it all on both sides, to be lionized as Fellini and idolized as Che. I wasn't alone in those dual ambitions. Many never outgrew them.

2 FROM SOUTH CAROLINA
BACKWARDS

I have only a dim memory of how I felt in August 1966, when—standing by the side of the road between Sumter and Myrtle Beach, South Carolina—I stared dumbstruck at the severed fourth finger of my left hand. I can't remember if blood was streaming from the stump as I stooped to pick the finger up with my good hand. I assume it was, though all I can be certain of is that I was trying not to faint and that the Southern cop opposite me had a terrified look on his face.

That cop may not have been older than I (I was twenty-two), but he was about a head taller and a lot broader. Only minutes before he had been pointing angrily past my wife Dyanne at Bruce Dinkins, the thirteen-year-old African-American kid in the back seat of the Corvair, demanding to know what "that boy" was doing in our car.

We were on the way to integrate the segregated bathhouses of Myrtle Beach, but I wasn't in a hurry to tell the cop that under the circumstances. Already I felt guilty about dragging young Bruce along on the enterprise. Dyanne and I had made him the lead in our student production of *A Raisin in the Sun*, and he regarded us as gods from the North, but this situation had spun out of control. Bruce probably blamed himself when the junior redneck dropped the jack at my feet.

We'd had a flat and, lacking our own jack, had flagged down a highway patrol car. The young cop had seemed happy to oblige us until noticing our racially mixed group. He turned surly, muttering, "Y'all do it yerself," with his eyes fixed on the young teenager. But I didn't know how to use the jack and had barely gotten it up when the whole car came down on my hand, breaking my finger off at the base.

Now Bruce was standing there watching one of his gods potentially

13

bleed to death. I urged the shell-shocked cop to drive me to the nearest hospital. "Don't get blood on my hat," he said, referring to the pristine Stetson on the seat beside him, as we barreled toward a small clinic in the town of Clinton. Dyanne waited with Bruce at the side of the road for a tow truck to come. When I got to the hospital, the receptionist asked for my address and emergency contact. I hesitated. The hospital was all white. Was it actually still segregated, I wondered? This could be a big mess. But I didn't have a choice. I told them to call the man who ran our program back in Sumter. I didn't bother to mention that he was the cousin of Martin Luther King.

I then slumped against the wall and nearly passed out, feeling as if I were living my own low-rent version of Edward Albee's play about the death of Bessie Smith. At least I was still alive, unlike Andy Goodman, my childhood best friend from New York's progressive Walden School. He'd been shot the previous year by the Ku Klux Klan in a racial incident that inspired the film *Mississippi Burning*. There hadn't been a day that summer when his murder was far from my mind.

Minutes later I was being wheeled into an operating room in that tiny clinic in rural South Carolina. I have never been religious, but I have a fleeting memory of saying a short prayer—before the anesthesia put my lights out—that the Southern doctor sewing my finger back on had been trained at some fancy out-of-state medical school.

Even though I'd had my occasional dreams of martyrdom-lite—being sprayed with power hoses, say, or even stung gingerly with cattle prods— an amputated finger was more than I'd bargained for. I'd signed up for the Yale Southern Teaching Program in the spring of 1966 full of ideal- istic images of Freedom Riders singing "We Shall Overcome." This was going to be the summer when I grew up socially and politically. After all, I was now a full-fledged civil rights worker, engaged in the greatest struggle of the era.

And for a while it had gone well. Dyanne and I had done our bits registering voters on rural black farms, teaching African-American his- tory to schoolkids in the "colored" part of Sumter and even organizing the first production (albeit truncated) in that part of the South of that seminal drama of black family life, *A Raisin in the Sun*. On weekends we would motor around neighboring states, once visiting the Student Non- Violent Coordinating Committee office in Atlanta in search of black history materials. There we ran into two of the more famous young idols of the period—Stokely Carmichael and Julian Bond. The exceptionally handsome and charismatic Bond—now president of the NAACP—was then making his first run for a congressional seat. He showed me a leaflet he planned to distribute to voters with the symbol of the Black Panther Party of Lowndes County, Alabama. It was the first time I had seen that famous sign of Black Power—though I had heard about it—and felt hurt when Bond rejected my offer to go precinct walking with him. He apparently didn't need a white boy in the black districts of Atlanta. I tried to understand. I had other things to do then, other ways I could serve the cause of racial equality.

This, however, was all cut short by my encounter with a redneck cop on my way to integrate Myrtle Beach. But was I actually the victim of a civil rights incident? Or had I just been a clumsy urban graduate student unable to operate a simple automobile jack without bringing the car down on my hand? What would I tell my friends and family when I got home? The whole affair was ambiguous.

My life before then had been more sheltered than I wanted to admit. Dartmouth College, where I had spent my undergraduate years, was a good school, but painfully far from the action at a time when I correctly surmised the world was about to go upside down. Dartmouth in those days wasn't even coed, a sure-fire prescription for social retardation, though at least I had a girlfriend at Skidmore.

I'd tried my best in high school to be ahead of the curve—wearing sunglasses, black turtleneck, and beret, in the emerging beatnik style—but the results were marginal. I was the youngest member of my Scarsdale High class and even being the first of them (probably) to smoke grass (with a local jazz musician who was teaching me to play the drums and called joints "medicated cigarettes") didn't amount to much. Nor did being the only one to witness Jack Kerouac reading live at Hunter College auditorium (circa 1959). My eyewitness tale of the Beat Generation icon slumped over the lectern, waving a bottle of Scotch while holding forth from the pages of *The Subterraneans* and beckoning the young Allen Ginsberg—then resembling a bespectacled yeshiva bocher from a road show *Fiddler on the Roof*—to join him on stage was of interest only to a tiny minority of like-minded Scarsdale High School classmates. We were the ones trying to be superficially cool, listening to Thelonious Monk and Gerry Mulligan on Symphony Sid's late night radio or, in the case of the folkie set, Joan Baez, but actually dreaming of normal teenage things like losing our virginity or getting into our college of choice.

I failed at the latter, only making the waiting list for Harvard, and just barely achieved the former before arriving at Dartmouth, having lost my cherry over summer vacation to what I thought was a desperately aging hooker (she could have been thirty) in a walk-up off the Place Clichy. *"J'ai un étudiant!"* she shouted as we climbed the stairs. At least she hadn't used the more demeaning *élève*, declaring me a student and not a "pupil." Perhaps she guessed I was college-bound.

Of course, this was still the very early Sixties—not yet what we've come to call "The Sixties." Dartmouth when I arrived had much the same atmosphere as Scarsdale High, though it was far from New York and its Greenwich Village Mecca, to which I would escape from the suburbs any chance I had in high school. The student body consisted of a lot of innocent jocks, a few nerds-before-their-time—mostly in the math department—and some preppies who didn't make it into Princeton. But there were exceptions; there always had been. My father had gone to Dartmouth and introduced me to his classmate Budd Schulberg '36 at a Yale game when I was about twelve. I knew even then this was the kind of Ivy graduate I aspired to be, assuming that I *would* graduate and not dare to go the full bohemian route like Scott Fitzgerald—to drop out (or *be* dropped out) in my junior year.

I searched out these eccentric types the moment I was on campus, but they were upperclassman and seemed inaccessible to me. One of them, Stephen Geller, cut a swashbuckling figure not only because he directed a production of *Waiting for Godot* and made his own student film (unheard of then), a burlesque of Bergman's *Seventh Seal*, but also because he came from *Los Angeles* and his father worked in *The Industry* (an arranger for Tennessee Ernie Ford, as it turned out). Geller knew people who actually *made* movies for a living, that weren't the doctors and lawyers or, worse yet, business people who had until then constituted nearly the entire panoply of adults in my life.

Somewhere in the second half of my freshman year, he and six others—a couple were attractive younger faculty wives, I was interested to note—staged the first ever nuclear disarmament demonstration in the history of the Ivy League in the middle of the Dartmouth Green. This was in the winter of 1960–1961, not long after the far more dramatic demonstrations in Berkeley, California, against the House Un-American Activities Committee (commemorated in the film *Operation Abolition*), which many consider the beginning of our modern era of protest. But I was more transfixed by the local New Hampshire event and yearned to participate.

Even then I realized on some instinctive level the important bond between progressive politics and artistic success, though I had no idea how intricate it was. But besides wanting to show my colors as an incipient progressive, the subject of the tiny Dartmouth demonstration had a rather large personal component for me. Nuclear weapons provided an eerie background to the childhood of most of my generation. And for me they were more than that. They were the major point of contention between my father and me, the focus of my adolescent rebellion.

My father, Norman Simon, was a radiologist—among the first in private practice in the City of New York—who volunteered his time for the Atomic Energy Commission. Although it was probably something of an exaggeration, I was told as a boy that my father would be de facto Governor of New York in the event of a nuclear attack. He had treated the "Hiroshima Ladies"—the group of victims of the Hiroshima blast who were flown to the U.S. for examination—and was supposed to know as well as anybody how to deal with the effects of radioactive fallout on the human body. When I was very young, he would spend many of his weekends at the Atomic Energy Commission installation in Oak Ridge, Tennessee, or at Los Alamos itself. (I have a dim recollection of being introduced to the Manhattan Project scientists Lisa Meitner and J. Robert Oppenheimer as a child. I must have been about three.) He would return from those weekends with a grim expression, having attended lectures on the latest doomsday weapons—by then they must have been thermonuclear—that only those with the highest security clearance were allowed to see.

My father's obtaining that elevated clearance provided the background for one of my more potent childhood memories. I recall at the age of seven standing in the lobby of our apartment, two blocks from New York's Mt. Sinai Hospital, where my father practiced, watching a pair of FBI agents conduct an interview about my dad. The agents were scary enough to me in their gangster-movie wide-brimmed fedoras, but not nearly as disturbing as the man they were questioning. He was the superintendent of our building, an angry drunk who beat his kid with an old-fashioned cat 'o nine tails. I knew this because his son Byron was my after-school playmate; I had seen the super whip him on more than one occasion in the shadows of the dank corridor near their basement apartment. I had also seen the welts on Byron's back and arms. The idea that a drunken thug like that super held my father's future in his hands was unnerving to my seven-year-old self. Nothing good could come of that. And my fears were only exacerbated by my pal and confidante Nick, our handsome young elevator man from the Bronx. He informed me that the feds had been asking if my dad was a commie. I knew for sure that he wasn't, but I wasn't certain what the elevator man thought, or anybody else for that matter. Those were paranoid times, even for a seven year old. And I couldn't ask anyone the truth at home. The atmosphere between my parents, never particularly relaxed, was extremely testy until that investigation was finally over and I somehow learned my father had the coveted "Q" clearance, whatever that meant.

So the old "duck and cover" game we used to play at PS 6 back in the early Fifties, hiding from atomic bombs with our heads in our hands while contorted under those cramped nineteenth-century folding school desks—that was a family matter to me. My fourth grade teacher, Mrs. Feig, whose husband was also a doctor, knew this. She'd announce to my classmates that "Roger's father" would come in to check up on them if they didn't behave in the proper manner during their proxy nuclear holocaust exercises.

I was proud of this parental recognition then, but by the time I was in junior high, adolescent hormones were kicking in and I was starting to separate from my father. I didn't like that he worked for the Atomic Energy Commission, and especially disliked that he often represented the AEC in debates with the newly formed Committee for a Sane Nuclear Policy. Never mind that my father told me not only that he actually sympathized with SANE but also that by the end of their debates everyone was really listening to *him*, because, after all, he knew the facts and they knew only their idealistic pronouncements. I wasn't buying. More than that—I was embarrassed. My father was on the wrong side.

Not long into high school, I was attending my first meetings—found in ads on the back of *The Village Voice*—of a short-lived group called the Student Peace Union. They advertised that they were a "Third Camp" in opposition to the foreign policies of the United States and the Soviet Union. I didn't realize then that the "Third Camp" consisted mostly of Trotskyists trying to find a way to rope in a few naive Quakers and other pacifists and put them on the straight and narrow to world socialism. In fact, at that point, I had no idea how to recognize any of the socialist sects or their methodologies or internecine rivalries. I wasn't even fifteen.

I came in from Scarsdale for the SPU lectures at the Judson Church with a high school friend whose parents *were* Quakers and members of the American Friends Service Committee. In reality my friend and I weren't very interested in the lectures. We wanted to meet the Village beatnik girls of our dreams. That meant we would skip out of the political speechifying after about ten minutes and head over to Rick's Café Bizarre or Rienzi's Coffee Shop on Bleecker in the hope of running into one, or preferably two, of those mysterious creatures in leotards. Of course, when we did, we suburban kids couldn't have been of less interest to them. So my friend and I ended up spending most of our time drinking hot cider (why was *that* hip?) and playing chess. Later, too young to go inside, we would "free beat" in front of Birdland, listening to Coltrane or Cannonball Adderley before taking the last train back to Westchester. A couple of times we even puffed on a joint late at night at the Scarsdale station. It seemed the safest place for such reckless abandon.

In true teenage fashion I resisted sharing these experiences with my parents, especially the furtive pot smoking. This was still the Fifties, remember. But I suspect that my mother romanticized my adventures anyway, thinking they were more than they were. (That would have been easy at that point.) She'd had literary dreams and I got some of my aspirations from her. Like seemingly half of my family, my mother had wanted to be a writer.

Ruth Simon—daughter of the Polish-born Ben Lichtenberg and the Bronx-born Minerva Kahn—dropped out of college in her junior year to take an assistant's job with the Paris branch of the *Chicago Tribune*. There she hung around Left Bank cafes and met journalistic lights like Walter

Lippman. It was a time in her life she told me about repeatedly when I was a boy—her trips to Spain after the Civil War and to Germany with the Nazis already in control. But as the Second World War loomed, she returned to America and, bourgeois impulses at work, agreed to marry my father after only a couple of dates. It helped that he was smart and good-looking (both my parents were attractive), but all the same he came from a seemingly lower-class Jewish family of Russian and Ukrainian immigrants from the mill town of Lawrence, Massachusetts and had to pass muster with my mother's more "aristocratic" father. Ben Lichtenberg was a foppish public relations man who admired Napoleon, dined frequently at the Pavillion, allegedly changed his Sulka's silk shirts five times a day and claimed to be related to the Baron von Lichtenberg—supposedly, or so my grandmother told me, one of the rare Jewish royals of the Austro-Hungarian Empire. (Google has nothing on this.)

After marrying, to keep her hopes of an independent career alive, my mother spent another couple of years as a publicist for classical musicians, during which time she walked around Manhattan wearing a hat fashioned from a long-playing record of Metropolitan Opera star Lili Pons. But after that, she never worked again. Later, I would live out those Paris literary dreams for her, but then, when I was in high school, hers were at their most thwarted. She was beginning to realize that she was staring down the barrel of forty years of stultifying suburban life out of a Cheever novel.

So my mother ameliorated her pain with a haze of prescription drugs. She was more or less addicted to tranquilizers and barbiturates throughout my high school years. My father the doctor kept the medicine cabinet well stocked, making it easy for her. I don't know if he was consciously medicating her, but it was certainly conventional for that generation to do this to themselves and sometimes to their children. The humorist S. J. Perelman was my father's patient, but it wasn't for that reason alone my father kept an autographed copy of *The Road to Miltown* on the living room coffee table. My generation's (and my) later much more public experiments with drugs don't seem so astonishing when juxtaposed with this secret reality of the Fifties, which sometimes bubbled to the surface in *New Yorker* cartoons. Maybe we were only making explicit what our parents had kept hidden.

Although my father came from that Orthodox immigrant home back in Lawrence, my parents' lifestyle, particularly in Scarsdale, was Jewish-WASP. They rarely went to synagogue or discussed religion at home; they liked to entertain formally and were members of a country club. Surfaces were of paramount importance. Even in the social sphere, things had to be dealt with in a decorous manner. My parents were Stevenson Democrats but I can't remember them actively lobbying for any political cause or even going to a meeting. Their involvement in the growing civil rights struggle was only peripheral. They sent me to visit family friends in Louisiana when I was thirteen, but when I returned, aghast, with my stories of "colored" water fountains and other Jim Crow horrors, they merely clucked their disapproval. They never did anything about it. The two exceptions came from my father's aforementioned professional interest in nuclear energy and his usually unspoken fascination with the Holocaust.

This kind of repressed behavior and hypocrisy is of course popularly associated with the Fifties. When, shortly after college, I read Yale psychologist Kenneth Kenniston's *The Young Radicals*—which defined the left-wing youth of my generation as being in rebellion against liberal parents who rarely acted on their values—I thought I'd found the academic version of my own autobiography. And for those days, I had. But the dialectic moves on and I had no idea how my view of my parents, particularly of my father, would circle back on itself. I am far more sympathetic to him now and recognize that his activities with the Atomic Energy Commission were in many ways heroic. He was a committed man in the sense that he believed that, on balance, the values of this country are positive and its role in the world necessary. He wanted to defend and protect it through his scientific work.

At that time, however, I was in Kenniston-style rebellion. By my sophomore year at Dartmouth I had become roommates with Alan Coggeshall, a tow-headed, angular character who resembled a latter-day Ichabod Crane and even came from Peekskill, New York, not far from Washington Irving's Sleepy Hollow. These were the days (1962) when we were first getting an inkling of the existence of psychedelic drugs and Alan, less risk-averse than I, would head off to Cambridge on weekends to participate in the early LSD experiments of Harvard psych professors Richard Alpert and Timothy Leary. When I listened to his tales of rainbows exploding to Bach cantatas, I never dreamed that Leary himself would be one of my closer friends in Hollywood in the Eighties, or that Alan would be dead the year after we graduated. He was in the back of a car that went flying off the road on its way to Bennington. I always assumed the driver was stoned, but don't know for sure.

What I do know is that Alan's LSD tales, fascinating though they were, made me nervous. Was I ready for explosions in my brain? Would I come back again? I remember feeling waves of apprehension when a package Alan had ordered arrived at our dorm room from Smith Cactus Farm in Laredo, Texas. It was peyote. Though the psychedelic cactus wasn't yet illegal, I could hardly believe it had actually arrived—dozens of scuzzy little dirt-covered buds inside a flimsy cardboard box wrapped in twine, all for about five dollars post paid. Save some die-hard Aldous Huxley fans, almost no one had heard of the plant then, in the early Sixties.

Among our minute group of incipient Dartmouth hipsters, however, a few were claiming already to have ingested the cactus. Eating it straight was supposed to be a one-way ticket to the vomitorium, so they said they'd either ground it into a paste for cookies or whirled it with ice cream and milk into a shake. One, an aspiring poet from West Virginia, had described his experience to me in glowing terms. Yes, he was sick for an hour or two and threw up all over the bathroom, and, yes, there was a period when all he could see were giant beetles coming out of his toilet...but then the visions...ah, the visions. He waved his hand at the transcendent magic of it all and gazed at me as if I were hopelessly square and hopelessly cowardly.

I didn't know whether to believe him or not, but he certainly had a point about my being scared. When the time came to turn on to our cactus stash, I pretended to eat while nipping tentatively at the skin of one of the buds as if the flesh beneath were imbued with rattlesnake venom, not mescaline. Then, when I thought no one was looking, I stuffed the cactus in my pocket. I waited until others began to report a "buzz" before nodding my concurrence. Yes, I said, those street lights outside our dorm *did* glow with incredible colors. The group clustered in our room that night was probably suspicious of me, but I just had to live with it. I wasn't ready for my first hallucinogenic trip and wouldn't be for some time to come.

Turned on or not, as my years at Dartmouth wore on, I felt increasingly isolated in Hanover, New Hampshire. Many of the more interesting upperclassmen like Geller had left and the world was changing at a rapid clip, the epicenter of the student universe moving west to Berkeley and the Free Speech Movement. By the time I entered the Yale Drama School in fall 1965, I was relieved to be in New Haven. There was a Berkeley girl in my playwriting class—Dyanne Asimow—and I quickly fell in love with her, knowing she would be a good companion in my growing desire to explore this new world and be part of the "My Generation," as the Who sang. And for a while, she was. But in those days, and in Hollywood especially, staying together wasn't easy.

3 MOSES WINE IS BORN

Recollecting the morning of September 11, 2001, I sometimes think that my fictional hero, my alter ego, detective Moses Wine, was among the tragic, desperate figures plunging down the façade of the World Trade Center. Even that day, I sensed it. The values and worldview of the left-wing hippie detective—the "stoned Sam Spade" as the *Los Angeles Times* called him years ago—had been battered practically beyond recognition, as had mine. I tried to explain this in my eighth Moses Wine novel, *Director's Cut*, but the book received the least attention and some of the most mediocre reviews of any I had written. Moses Wine's fans didn't want a revised Moses—at least a fair percentage of them didn't.

I owed a lot to Moses, and still do. I had invented him almost on a whim twenty-nine years before that September, sitting in my backyard in the Echo Park district of Los Angeles, sharing a joint with Alan Rinzler. It was like a scene from some Sergeant Pepper rerun—two lost Jewish members of the Beatles, me with a John Lennon beard and long, scraggly (but already prematurely thinning) hair, Alan with an Afro *à la* Abbie Hoffman or Dylan—giggling from marijuana.

Inside, I wasn't so happy. Alan, the editor of my first two novels, was rejecting my third. He had just become the head of Straight Arrow Books, the new publishing arm of *Rolling Stone*, and his "business guy" had said my latest effort—a grim, Simenon-like tale of an anti-Castro Cuban in LA kidnapping the child of the radical lawyer next door on the anniversary of the Bay of Pigs—was not commercial. No doubt his "business guy" was right. I knew it even then. Alan felt guilty, however. We were friends, and he didn't want to reject me. The other books I'd done for him were successful, relatively, anyway. And the Cuban one might have been better written than the previous two books. But this time he was working for a new publisher. Indeed, he was almost the publisher himself, as long as he stayed in the good graces of Jann Wenner, the young and ambitious founder of *Rolling Stone* and the *real* publisher in this instance. He had to think as a businessman, albeit a stoned one—not much of a contradiction in those days.

"Couldn't you do something more *Rolling Stone*?" he asked me. If only I could, I thought. At that moment I was pretty close to broke. No Hollywood jobs. No novel. Two little kids and a wife, and no prospects. My father's warnings about going to medical school as a backup were sounding all too accurate. But then something came out of me in a rush, something I'd never thought of before. "Y'know," I said, "I've been reading a lot of detective novels lately ... Ross Macdonald, Raymond Chandler...maybe I could do a detective for our generation...Left-wing, hippie-ish ... smokes hash instead of drinks booze ... "

Alan's eyes lit up. "Wow, that's great!" he said, "How fast can you do it...? And what do you want to call your dick?" "Moses Wine," I said, equally impetuously. That was the name of the protagonist in an autobiographical novel I'd been playing with, for lack of anything better to do.

"Perfect," Alan said. Then he added, "Make him divorced, with kids," already identifying with the character.

About six weeks later I had written *The Big Fix*, which became a bestseller. It has been published in a half dozen editions in the U.S. since and in over a dozen languages. It also jump-started my Hollywood career and was made into a movie starring Richard Dreyfuss, for which I did the script. I wrote seven more "Moses Wine" books, which won awards in the U.S. and abroad, and made me friends in many countries.

In other words, it changed my life. Now I was the guy who wrote the radical hippie detective. Sometimes I liked the idea. Sometimes I wished I did something else, something with more apparent gravitas. Why not make films *à la* Antonioni, perhaps, or write fat, impenetrable novels in the style of Gaddis—or anyone else whose books appeared on the front page of the *New York Times Book Review*, not on the back pages under "Crime." But Moses Wine was what I was most identified with for many years, and it wasn't so bad. I'm not going to go on here about the ever-shifting line between popular and serious fiction, or about whether Edmund Wilson was correct in his attack on the mystery genre in "Who Cares Who Killed Roger Ackroyd?" It was never an argument that interested me, except in the areas of pride and ego. I didn't like being in the back of the bus. But intellectually I was and am bored by the question. If Wilson didn't like mysteries, that's fine with me. I've always preferred Graham Greene to Edmund Wilson anyway.

My strategy for writing *The Big Fix*, and the Moses Wine novels in general, was a simple one. I just selected a crime I thought relevant, put myself in the role of detective, and used as much of myself as possible, pulling in as many details from my personal life and times as I could. I never really outlined the books, just made them up as I went along, "taught myself the story," as Gore Vidal described his own process. I didn't even always know "whodunit" in advance. In first person detective fiction, I told myself, this was a superior technique, since it put the author in the emotional and psychological position of the detective, baffled by the crime and trying to figure it out until the end. It would also add spontaneity. Privately, however, I was embarrassed and insecure about my casual approach until, a few years on, while appearing on a panel for aspiring writers with Tony Hillerman—then considered a master of the genre for his books starring Navajo detective Jim Chee—I was asked the question of questions: "Do you outline your stories or do you make them up as you go along?" On the spot in front of an audience of perhaps two hundred with a tape recorder going, I could not tell a lie. "I make them up as I go along," I admitted. The unexpected sigh of relief next to me came from the multiple-award-winning Hillerman. He did, too, he told the audience, who appeared confused by these surprise admissions from supposed professionals in the form. This was not what they had learned in school.

Of course, the secret to my thrillers was that I stayed as close as possible to the zeitgeist. Indeed, that was easy, because the impulse to make an impact on the affairs of the day was what propelled my desire to do the Moses Wine series in the first place. In a way, it was my first, bizarre entry into blogging—blogging with a plot, you might call it. *The Big Fix*, as an example, was written at the height of the McGovern campaign of 1972, for which I was walking precinct. I simply turned the bland peacenik McGovern into the bland peacenik Miles Hawthorne and changed the background from a presidential to a California senatorial campaign. (Ah, fiction!) For the mystery premise, I had Hawthorne (McGovern) being smeared, his campaign endangered, by the backing of Howard

Eppis—an Abbie Hoffman-style renegade who was making statements to the effect that Hawthorne was the man finally to bring the dreamed-of revolution to capitalist America.

Moses Wine was brought into the case to find this Eppis, if indeed it really was Eppis, by his old Berkeley girlfriend Lila Shea, now a Hawthorne campaign worker. ("The last time I saw Lila Shea," it began, "we were making love in the back of a Chevy hearse across from the Oakland Induction Center. Tear gas was going off in our ears.... etc.") My Moses doesn't care much for Hawthorne (too middle-of-the-road), but Lila is killed not long after they see each other again and he takes the case to avenge her death. Classic detective stuff, with a Sixties spin.

I had no idea how well it was going to work. I was just having fun. Partly for that reason, I brought in the character of Aunt Sonya—a wise-acre Jewish great aunt with a socialist-anarchist background straight out of the Yiddishe bund—as a kind of sidekick and conscience to Moses not to stray from the radical line. (In the movie version, she joked about her romantic relations with Bakunin. "He was a very good dancer," she said.) I never had such an aunt, but in those days I think I wished I had. I came from that Jewish-WASP background and to me the old socialists, closer to my wife Dyanne's family but still distant even from them, were warmer, more authentic people, *haymishe* in the Yiddish expression.

When I look at this from a contemporary perspective, my move toward neoconservative politics stems, in part, anyway, from a similar impulse. I wanted to join those former Trotskyites—the Podhoretzes and the Kristols—in what I imagined to be their *haymishe* pro-democracy world. Of course, I never would have conceived of this odyssey when writing *The Big Fix*. In those days I worried whether I was radical enough. Was I a sell-out, taking advantage of my lefty friends and connections? Ironically, years later, when I became a friend of John Podhoretz, the scion of the neocon family and his father's successor as the editor of *Commentary*, he told me that the Moses Wine books were the only left-wing literature of our generation that he could stand. He identified with the character, and with his humor, in spite of himself.

Even before it was published, *The Big Fix* was given a boost by Ross Macdonald (the pen name of Kenneth Millar) who was then the dean of American detective fiction and on the cover of *Newsweek*. Phillip Handler, a professor of mine at Dartmouth, had passed the manuscript to a friend of his who was friends with Millar/Macdonald. I was in awe of Macdonald, preferring his work even to Chandler and Hammett's for its more intellectually complex Freudian underpinnings. I assumed that he wouldn't be impressed with my pastiche. I couldn't have been more wrong. Not only did he admire my work, he gave it the most extraordinary send-off imaginable, calling it a revolution in the field. I haven't had a comparable experience in my professional life to when I first opened that letter from Ken, not even the day I found out I was nominated for an Academy Award for the screenplay of *Enemies: A Love Story*. *The Big Fix*, after all, was all mine; Moses Wine was all mine. And I knew that, with his backing, it would be noticed.

Several weeks later I drove up to meet Millar at his home in Santa Barbara. When I arrived, he was waiting in the courtyard of the El Patio Mexican Restaurant wearing a black Borsalino. I was wearing a similar hat, signature apparel for detective writers, as if we'd modeled ourselves on film noir characters and belonged to the famous LAPD Hat Squad circa 1940. Millar greeted me like an old friend. Of all the writers I've ever met, Ken was the most generous with his colleagues. Unlike the many authors who denigrate their competition, sometimes viciously, he made an effort to encourage young talent and even to buck up older veterans after years of failure.

I saw this often at that El Patio Restaurant, where I'd go every month for the writers' lunch grouped around Ken. The pain he'd endured in his personal life made this generosity of spirit all the more impressive. (He and author Margaret Millar's only child was a disturbed young woman who, like one of the disappearing children in Ken's own novels, ran away from home and spent time in Camarillo State Mental Hospital before dying of a brain hemorrhage at thirty-one.) There was a nobility to the man similar to the honorable knight critics and readers found in his protagonist Lew Archer. I didn't quite realize it then, but when Ken wrote of my work that I was "the most brilliant new writer of private detective fiction who has emerged in some years" and that "*The Big Fix*, like *The Big Sleep*, should become something of a landmark in its field," he was giving me a gift that would ensure the book's success with good reviews, foreign translations, and literary prizes.

Those prizes included that year's Best First Mystery from the Crime Writers of Great Britain, a group traditionally unfriendly to American authors. Hugely flattered, I flew to London for the awards banquet. Also in attendance was my actor friend Richard Dreyfuss, who, after many ups and downs, would play Moses Wine in *The Big Fix* movie six years later.

Richard, who had just made his first sensation at twenty-four in *American Graffiti*, was in London playing the lead in an art film. He sat in the back of the banquet room, calling attention to himself by breaking in on the proceedings *sotto voce*. The fusty British authors on the dais were clearly put off, and I was embarrassed. Richard was there at my behest. Soon enough, the self-aggrandizement was mercifully over and I accepted the award from Dick Francis, the dean of British crime writers and the author of dozens of horse racing mysteries. I remember that he introduced me as a soon-to-be "old lag," British parlance for someone who writes workmanlike thrillers year after year and then goes to his grave. Was this what I wanted to be? The room seemed to be full of them. I had more interest in Dreyfuss, despite his narcissistic outbursts and even though I knew that dealing with movie stars like him would be complicated at best.

What I didn't realize is that years later Richard and I—then comrades, as he came from a socialist background—would be on differing sides politically, although in Richard's case those differences would be nuanced. Unlike like many actors, he was an intelligent man who actually read books before he spouted off. But what I was watching back then in London was a need for the limelight under any circumstances—a need that almost always carries through for actors. In those days, this wasn't a problem for me, because many of those actors identified with Moses Wine, wanted to be seen as the "hero of the people," especially if that hero was a private dick who acted heroically and got the girls.

Of course, not everyone liked *The Big Fix*. I got my biggest pushback from those "girls," more specifically "women," because the book was published in 1973, when the Women's Liberation Movement was sweeping the intelligentsia. It had hit my own household with a vengeance. Dyanne was a founding member of one of the first women's consciousness-raising groups in LA, probably in the country. Most members of the group were in the media and film—among them journalist Marcia Seligson, filmmaker Lynne Littman (who made the 1983 anti-nuke melodrama *Testament*), and graphic artist Sheila Levrant de Bretteville, who helped establish the Women's Building in downtown Los Angeles. They met weekly in one of the women's homes, including ours, and I remember listening to their conversations from the second floor balcony, a male spy on the women's movement, nervous that I'd fall off and make a spectacle of myself.

Some of these consciousness-raising discussions were earnest and theoretical, but the more interesting ones contained personal gossip about the women themselves and the men in their lives—who was sleeping with whom, who was a male chauvinist pig or a philanderer, and what the women themselves were up to. And everyone was up to a lot. This was the era when sexual liberation was in the air and monogamy challenged as a form of male oppression or just old-fashioned bourgeois repression. Whatever the case, sexual politics and plain old ordinary sex of the libidinal variety were getting mixed up as never before.

This got more intense when a men's consciousness-raising group was formed as a rejoinder to the women's group, in a fit of what might be described as vagina envy. If the women could get together and dish, the men could, too—so long as they couched it in the self-abnegating rhetoric of the era. Along with me in this partly self-lacerating but superficially political endeavor was a similar group of young and ambitious LA artsy types, including the soon-to-be directors Rob Cohen (*The Fast and the Furious*) and Taylor Hackford (*An Officer and a Gentleman*, married then to Lynne Littman in the women's group, now to Helen Mirren), architect Peter de Bretteville (married to Sheila Levrant de Bretteville), the photographer Ben Lifson (married to poetess Martha Lifson in the women's group), painter Lance Richbourg, and lawyer Tom Pollack, who was then the attorney of wunderkind George Lucas and one day would be the head of Universal Studios. We seemed to be a high-powered cabal in the making, paying ritual obeisance to breaking the shackles of male chauvinism.

Well, not completely. What soon evolved is that Ben Lifson was having an open affair (open to us, anyway) with the girlfriend of one of the youngest men in our group. His name was Steve—I can't remember his surname, but that's just as well—and he happened to be a photography student of Lifson's at Cal Arts. This was all a subject of constant men's group discussion. "Open marriage" was trendy then and we had before us a living, breathing example of it. Within a few weeks, however, all theory was going out the window as the sordidness of the reality set in. Members of the group justifiably grew to hate Ben and to pity the pathetic Steve. I say pathetic because he went along with this without doing the natural thing—kicking Ben in the balls—while justifying his inaction in the now comical ideological rhetoric of the period.

Against this background I began to conceive *Wild Turkey*, the second Moses Wine novel, which was deliberately more comic than its predecessor. People had told me *The Big Fix* was funny. That was news to me, but I accepted it, nodding as if the humor was intentional. It may be that the best comedy *is* unintentional—it's simply the honest observation of reality. But for the next book, I decided to be more overt about it.

At the beginning of the new novel, Moses—who'd become a minor celebrity from his *Big Fix* adventure—is burst in on at three in the morning by Dr. Gunther Thomas, a not very well disguised version of Hunter Thompson, the 'gonzo' journalist and author of *Fear and Loathing in Las Vegas*. Dr. Thomas wants to do a profile of the "hippie Sam Spade" for *Rolling Stone*. He's even got a case for Wine. The best-selling author Jock Hecht—a Norman Mailer-type who has written a notorious book on sexual freedom—is wanted for the murder of the anchorwoman on a TV morning news program. He needs someone to help get him off. Trouble is, Moses's "ex" is in India with her guru and has left him with their young kids, one of who is still in diapers (the Women's Lib angle!) and constantly in need of a change. Undeterred, Dr. Gunther Thomas grabs Moses and the kids, and off we go.

The plot, as it is with these stories, is intentionally convoluted, but suffice it to say that Jock Hecht himself is murdered in short order. Moses is hired by Jock's attractive widow, Nancy, who reveals (shades of the men's consciousness group) that she and Jock had had an open marriage. It had been Jock's idea, with Nancy going along grudgingly. She and Moses are kindred spirits in that regard. They both recoil from open marriage, but feel guilty or a little square or a combination of the two for being so conventional. Naturally, they fall for each other, but due to the conventions of the genre, their romance is not to be.

Reflecting on this today, with the perspective of over three decades, it's hard to believe that we were all so naïve about marriage. (It's not hard to believe, however, that this story attracted Warren Beatty—but more on that later.) Basing human relationships on ideology is almost comically absurd and most often a convenient lie. But I did enjoy writing—and, yes, I admit, to researching—the scenes set at a sexual freedom "institute" in Topanga Canyon—the same one (Sandstone) that had been the basis for Gay Talese's notorious "new journalist" studies of American mores.

It's fair to ask me whether I participated personally in the "open marriage" experiment of the time. To be honest, I didn't have the guts, even if I wanted to—and I didn't want to, in the end. But that didn't mean I was honest with my spouse or she with me. Perhaps influenced by the temper of the times, or just by our own characters, we did cheat on each other. As the Wine books and, consequently, my movie career, were mushrooming, my wife and one of my best friends—both of whom were writers, but frustrated in their careers—were having a long and involved affair. Of course, envy wasn't their only motivation. I was plenty to blame myself. But by the Eighties, my marriage with Dyanne Asimow, from which we had two beautiful children, was dead. I was on my way as a grown man to live out the experiences most have as a teenager or young adult. I would be married again, this time for only a short while, and then have numerous relationships—sometimes telling myself it was for art—before winding up married a third time, happily and permanently. In a way, the Wine books can be looked upon as a hidden journal of my three marriages and those relationships.

All this was life imitating art imitating life imitating …For a while I was too busy living this out to write the book, so my editor Alan Rinzler, anxious to get a sequel published, invited me up to San Francisco to finish it. He locked me in the same room at the Seal Rock Inn where Hunter Thompson had just completed *his* latest book for Straight Arrow. We shared the same cleaning lady, who would come into the room while I banged away on my Selectric, look into the bathroom, and say, shaking her head, "Mr. Thompson—he had so many pills in that cabinet." No doubt.

The only other visitor I had was Alan, who showed up early each evening for the pages (I was trying to knock out about ten per day), peruse them, and then work with me on where the next part of the story was headed. This reminded me of the way Hollywood "scribes" were said to have worked in the Thirties and Forties, passing the pages under the door to cigar-chomping producers. (Alan smoked joints incessantly.) One result of having an editor with me on a daily basis may have been that *Wild Turkey* (named for the bourbon swilled by the Hunter Thompson character) has the most carefully wrought plot of any of my books. I know this because it was so easy to adapt into a screenplay. I have personally worked on a film version of three of my books—*The Big Fix, The Straight Man,* and *Wild Turkey*—and *Turkey* worked most perfectly because of its tight plotting, an indispensable element of good screenwriting. At one point I expected *Wild Turkey* to be completed first, even though *The Big Fix* was the earlier book and had been under option already.

When *The Big Fix* came out, there was an immediate flutter of Hollywood attention. Mike Gruskoff, a classic movie producer with roots in the garment business, took the book to Twentieth Century Fox and the studio optioned it for the hot new director of the time—Martin Scorsese. I'd seen his groundbreaking *Mean Streets,* which I considered the best film by a new American director in years, and was thrilled. How could this be happening to *me*?

Well, it didn't. I met with Marty, who seemed standoffish—curious, considering that he'd signed up to direct. After a few weeks he drifted out of contact. It turned out that something better—in his eyes, at least—had come up; he was off directing *Alice Doesn't Live Here Anymore* with Ellen Burstyn. Gruskoff and I were left on our own. He suggested another director—a kid named Steven Spielberg who'd just made a television movie (*Duel*) everybody liked. He was supposedly interested in my book. I scoffed. How could this person, younger than I was by two or three years and a *television* (snort!) director to boot, understand the political nuances of my revolutionary novel? I remember having several arguments about this with Gruskoff, who—for some misguided reason—thought that I was being belligerent and selfish. What'd he know? He was a dumb producer from the *schmatta* business, no less. Besides, in my heart of hearts, I thought *I* should direct the movie. Who was this Spielberg? Soon enough, Stephen had drifted away as well, leaving Mike and me to develop the script on our own. It was never made. Within two years, Spielberg had directed both *Jaws* and *Close Encounters of the Third Kind*.

Looking back, I think I must have been an arrogant idiot to pass up what could have been a life-changing opportunity. (It wasn't the only time that happened. Years later I told my agent I had no interest in adapting the dull novel that had been submitted to me—*Forrest Gump*.) But Hollywood is like that: halfway between the stock market and Las Vegas. You're never sure where you stand and when to jump in or out.

And I *did* get a second chance. Just after *Wild Turkey* was published, there was another round of buzz. Someone even told me that Warren Beatty was showing up at parties with a copy of my book in his hip pocket, telling people he wanted to play the lead. Flattering though it was, that seemed strange to me. The very WASP-y Beatty didn't seem like much of a fit with the Jewish Moses Wine (I'd imagined Dreyfuss from the start), and in those days I had no idea Beatty was remotely political. I still saw him as the pretty boy who made his mark opposite Natalie Wood in *Splendor in the Grass* and then continued to amass a long list of equally glamorous leading ladies. In any event, nothing happened and that gossip disappeared into the great maw of the movie business when Warner Brothers bought the rights to *Wild Turkey* for producer Gene Corman, brother of the notorious Roger Corman of low-budget horror fame.

I worked on a script for Gene, which, to my surprise and pleasure, the studio actually liked on its first submission. Everything moved swiftly. Gene, the Warners executive in charge of the project, and I agreed that Richard Dreyfuss should play Moses. Richard was living in Malibu then, not working. I heard the studio was about to make him a "pay-or-play" offer (usually a guarantee of production, as they didn't want to "pay" *without* the "play") of $500,000—a decent fee in 1975. I also heard that Richard was primed to accept it. All that we needed was the final okay from former agent Ted Ashley, who was then CEO of Warners.

It never came. The script was placed in the dreaded "turn-around," a process by which the studio returns the now tarnished screenplay to the producer to find financing elsewhere—not an easy thing, since the original studio usually attaches onerous inflated costs. Corman, however, was determined to get my script done, convincing me against my better judgment to bowdlerize my work in the time-honored Hollywood tradition. First we made Moses Wine *not* Jewish (Jewish characters were generally considered a no-no, despite the large number of Jews in the Industry), then *not* a detective (there were too many detective movies—we made him city attorney); then we moved the locale from Los Angeles to Atlanta. None of this worked, as acts of desperation rarely do.

The whole affair made me depressed and ornery, so, again in the time-honored Hollywood tradition, I blamed my agent. At this point it was William Morris, but I had several suitors, including Ziegler Ross and Adams, Ray & Rosenberg, both known as respected "literary" agencies. (I put that in quotes because what passed for literary in Hollywood would set eyes rolling in Manhattan. They were the best of a dubious crop.) The Morris office knew that I was ready to jump and asked what they could do for me. I said that whatever it was, they should do it soon, because I was considering other options.

They were aware of Warren Beatty's interest in my books. He was a William Morris client, so I had an appointment with him almost immediately; as luck would have it, he lived in a penthouse at the top of the Beverly Wilshire Hotel, only a moment's walk from William Morris.

I don't remember my heart thumping as I rode up the private elevator at the Wilshire, but it surely must have been. It's hard to fix dates so long ago, but it had to have been late 1975 or early 1976, as you will see. The elevator opened on Beatty's apartment, which, though it was supposed to be a penthouse, didn't seem remotely like one. It was a dank place, books and scripts scattered about, making it more like the home of a messy grad student than of a movie star. Warren, who was sitting in the middle of this jumble in his shirtsleeves, gestured for me to enter. He was on the phone but was off quickly and flashed the charismatic smile that the world knew well from the movies.

Beatty's "star wattage" was at its peak, thanks to a virtually unbroken line of hits from *Bonnie and Clyde* to *McCabe & Mrs. Miller*, *Shampoo* and *The Parallax View*. I am not the first to note this, but encounters with Beatty are almost always a form of seduction. In the case of men, he goes for your talent. He had read my work and was aware of my leftism, obviously, but I was still surprised that the first thing out of his mouth after saying hello was whether I knew who John Reed was. Sure, I quickly replied, mentioning *Ten Days That Shook the World*, Reed's seminal 1919 work on the Russian Revolution, as if I had read it. I hadn't. Well, Beatty continued, he was planning on directing and starring in a biographical movie about Reed and his relationship to Louise Bryant—the Marxist/anarchist and proto-feminist glamour girl of journalism. It'd be an epic of romance, politics, and revolution. He was planning on picking a screenwriter soon, and wanted to know if I was interested. It was between Paddy Chayevsky and me.

At that point the phone rang again. I was relieved; if it hadn't, I might have fainted. Forget Moses Wine and the horse he rode in on. There was nothing I could have imagined wanting to write more than this, though I knew that Chayevsky—the author of *Marty*, *The Americanization of Emily*, and *Hospital*—meant stiff, probably impossible, competition.

The call turned out to be from Jimmy Carter. That's how I can recall that this meeting took place in late 1975 to early 1976; Carter was just launching his run for the presidency. I listened as the Southern governor kowtowed and kissed up to the movie star in search of his support, which obviously meant money and a significant endorsement, also entrée into the liberal Hollywood crowd. The name "Jack" was mentioned. Warren seemed to be enjoying the exchange and was acting out a bit for my benefit. This was my first brush with the Hollywood-Washington nexus, which is now a commonplace.

When he hung up, Beatty asked if I thought Carter would make a good president. I don't remember my answer, but I probably equivocated. (Now I would just snort.) I was far more interested in my own advancement, and I didn't want to disturb that possibility with any rash statements. Beatty didn't do much to tip his hand either. As I later learned, that was typical Warren. He played footsie with politicians the same way he played footsie with potential film collaborators (and, needless to say, girlfriends), relishing his power until he made a decision based on a timetable known only to him—and probably not even to him. The same ambivalence has been apparent in his own tentative steps into electoral politics, when he's been touted for the California governorship or the Senate, and has publicly played with the idea and then backed away. I was never surprised. He is far too much of a control freak to tolerate the hurly-burly of politics, in which it's highly difficult to regulate your press in the way a movie star of his stature is used to doing. And he was more obsessive about that than most of them. This is a man who definitely only wants to be photographed one way.

To be fair, Warren was the only person on the Hollywood Left who has ever impressed me with his knowledge of radical politics. That's not necessarily saying much, but he was familiar with the finer points of theory to a degree that would have left most of his entertainment industry colleagues—and probably some college professors—glassy-eyed. I heard years later that his name appears on the checkout list for several arcane texts about socialist history—works on the Third International and such—at Harvard's Widener Library. Does that mean he really read them? No, but I suspect that he may have while writing *Reds*, the movie he was dreaming that day we met in the mid-Seventies. *Reds*, his highly romantic version of the John Reed–Louise Bryant story, finally reached the theaters in 1981, with Warren playing Reed and Diane Keaton as Bryant. Beatty won the Oscar for directing the film. Its Oscar-nominated screenplay is credited to Beatty and British playwright Trevor Griffiths—no Roger Simon *or* Paddy Chayevsky in sight.

I may have lost my chance at writing it a few days after that first meeting. I received a phone call from Warren out of the blue asking whether my wife and I would like to go out to dinner that night with him and "Michelle." By Michelle I knew he meant his main squeeze "Mama" Michelle Phillips of the Mamas and the Papas. Dyanne and I had another engagement that night, to go to a spiritualist "table tapping" (calling forth of ancestors) with our friend the anthropologist Barbara Myerhoff. (Barbara apparently believed in such things.) Careerist that I was, I was more than willing to cancel and dine with Warren and Michelle. Dyanne wasn't, and insisted, for whatever reason, that we honor our obligation to Barbara. I remember fighting about this, claiming that the "table tapping" was nonsense, anyway, but Dyanne wouldn't relent. Off we went to the tapping, which was, indeed, even sillier than one could imagine. Warren didn't call me again for several years.

I was with another woman when I first saw *Reds* in 1981. She was the producer Renee Missel, who would become my second wife. We were at a very romantic point and she thought the Reed-Bryant story was about us, metaphorically, anyway. I don't know if I was so sure, caught up as I was in very conventional bourgeois feelings of guilt about leaving my first wife and children—though almost all of that guilt was about the children. As for Warren, he, of course, never played Moses Wine. By that time, *The Big Fix* had already been a successful film starring Richard Dreyfuss.

Considering all the ups and downs of the previous attempts to make a Moses Wine film, the production of *Fix*, as it was called on the set, came about relatively easily. I'd stayed in touch with Dreyfuss, who'd always wanted to do the character. By 1978 or so, his power in the business had reached the level of a "bankable" actor, someone with so much box office clout that he could pretty much pick his project, as long as it wasn't a dramatization of the phone book. (With some "bankable" actors, like Beatty in those days, it could *be* the phone book: "So, Warren, are we talking the Yellow Pages or the White Pages?") Richard and I got together with his buddy Carl Borack—a commercials producer who would take the lead in the production area—and formed the Moses Wine Company. We took the package to Universal, where Richard had made *Jaws*, through Verna Fields, the film's editor, who had gone on to become a studio executive. Verna, everybody's den mother, passed it on to Ned Tanen, the head of Universal.

It was an easy sell, not only because of Richard but also because Ned identified with Moses Wine. I was at first astonished that a rich and powerful studio chief could identify with a hippie detective living in a working-class and Chicano barrio of LA. But it didn't take me long to understand that I had created a kind of mirror for people's counter lives. A studio head was in his soul a down-at-the-heels gumshoe out to buck the system and to save the poor and downtrodden. Never mind that he was experiencing these feelings in a multi-million-dollar ocean-view home in Pacific Palisades, a home adorned with museum-quality Navajo rugs. Ned was married at the time to Kitty Hawks, the daughter of director Howard Hawks and fashion icon Slim Keith (later Lady Keith)—not exactly the company Moses Wine traveled in.

I didn't realize it then, but I was witnessing one of the first cases I would see of the bifurcated Hollywood personality. In Ned Tanen's case it was relatively benign, because he had a sense of irony about his position. In many other cases it was far less so.

The studio left me alone with Dreyfuss for the writing of the film. In fact, I was treated remarkably well by them the entire time, contrary to the fables of Hollywood's cruelty to writers. Part of this was that the star protected me, but it was also because I had written the book and they had heard of it. I wasn't *just* a screenwriter. I was a novelist who might not even need them. (I learned to encourage the studio executives' belief that I earned much more money from my books than I did; it made them insecure about their hold on me. It was a lie, of course. I badly needed the screenwriting money to support my family.)

Even then, novelists in Hollywood were a diminishing number. Most of the writers were film school grads using their screenwriting as a wedge to get a directing assignment. This didn't make for exceptional writing. It's not by accident that the films from the Golden Era were better written—many of them by Broadway playwrights.

More surprisingly, the studio didn't interfere with the film politically, to the extent that the roll-up at the end shows Moses Wine marching off away from camera, his arms around his young children, jocularly teaching them to sing the "Internationale," as if this were the way any All-American dad would behave. This was never mentioned in any of the reviews—most of which were favorable—nor did anyone at the studio ever speak of it to me or anyone else I know of. It was also never referred to in the numerous market research cards turned in by the audiences in two large preview screenings in San Jose and Denver. Perhaps no one recognized it—or, if they did, they didn't want to say.

The script was peppered with liberal-left one-liners, including references to the Russian anarchist Bakunin that couldn't possibly have meant anything to 99.9 percent of the audience. Some of these were added immediately before shooting because Dreyfuss broke his wrist in an accident a month before the start date. We had the choice to shut down and wait until he healed or to write something that would cover his character being a private dick with his arm in a cast. We chose the latter, and I was able to turn this into a plus with some liberal wisecracks Moses makes whenever he's asked about his fractured arm ("Bar fight with a Bircher"). The truth is revealed at the end: It was just a dopey accident from trying to learn to skateboard from his kids.

Dreyfuss, Jeremy Kagan (the film's director, brought on pretty late in the game), and I shared the film's politics—in retrospect, a rather sentimental vision of the Sixties as seen from the late Seventies. One scene shows Dreyfuss looking at television clips of the old days—Chicago 1968—with tears of nostalgia in his eyes. This wasn't particularly my kind of thing—and I resisted writing it—but it played well with the audience. Much of Hollywood politics is at root sentimental. It's about feeling good about yourself without having to do much more than sound off—or make a "touching" scene in a movie. My heart (and writing) was even then more in black comic *mockery* of the Sixties, as in the scene when the Abbie Hoffman–Jerry Rubin character is revealed to have turned very comfortably into a bourgeois ad man while supposedly in hiding as a dangerous underground revolutionary.

Richard, whose father was a socialist, and Jeremy, whose father was a rabbi, were more emotional about those days, although I undoubtedly participated in radical politics more directly than they did. One of the more effective scenes in *The Big Fix* movie, when Moses goes inside LA County jail to obtain information from the Linkers (Yiddish for "leftists"), a couple based on Bill and Emily Harris of Symbionese Liberation Army fame, came from my own experience with the Harrises only a few years before.

Not long after they were arrested for kidnapping Patty Hearst, I received a phone call from the producer Tamara Asseyev—who would eventually co-produce *Norma Rae*—asking if my wife Dyanne and I would like to write an as-told-to book about the radical couple. Tamara somehow had the rights to this. The Harrises liked the idea because it would be a couple writing about a couple and because their lawyer, Leonard Weinglass of the Chicago 8 trial, was a friend of mine and had vouched for us. Dyanne and I went down to the jail in the LA County Courthouse with Lenny to visit Bill and Emily, who were allowed to meet us together behind a wire-mesh window. At first they struck me as a rather banal pair, though she was somewhat brighter and more attractive than he was. All the same, I was apprehensive about consorting with them, not least because they were making "revolutionary" demands about editorial control of our writing. This was particularly disconcerting since they kept talking about furthering the revolution through "our" book, using the ideas of their leader, Cinque Mtume—most of which "ideas" were an Africanized version of socialism derived from something called the Seven Principles of Kwanzaa. They were represented in the hydra-headed cobra symbol of the SLA.

I didn't know how I could write that book, even though my agent, Owen Laster, assured me at the outset it would be a best-seller. The Harrises—"Teko" and "Yolanda" in their *noms de guerre*—were the most famous criminals on the planet at that point, second in notoriety only to Patty "Tania" Hearst herself. But I kept brooding about how their SLA friends had shot to death the Oakland School Superintendent Marcus Foster, an African-American, and badly wounded his deputy merely because Foster wanted to give students in his district identification cards. To whom had the Harrises been listening, to accept something like that—even if they hadn't done it themselves? Cinque must have been one charismatic guy. Or were Bill and Emily just extremely gullible?

They seemed that way to me. What surprised me talking to them was how new their radical politics were; it'd only been a couple years since they arrived in California as innocents from the Midwest. It was as if they came to Berkeley, heard all the rhetoric at some Marxist reading group, believed it without question, and went out and bought guns. They didn't realize that for most people in those groups, bourgeois students and intellectuals, "revolution" is talk—a parlor game played over Gauloises and cappuccino, as it has been for decades. To Bill and Emily, it was brand new. They thought: that makes sense, let's do it now! And off they went, kidnapping and robbing banks for the good of the people, following their leader Cinque in what seemed like a monumental case of Stockholm Syndrome. Patty Hearst certainly had one, in their telling. On our second visit, Bill and Emily recounted how one day they'd gone hiking with Patty in Tilden Park and the heiress had gotten stuck on a ledge. A policeman had to help her get free, but she didn't tell him a thing about who she was—just walked off with Bill and Emily. They were gleeful about that.

Now *that* I wanted to put in the book, but the whole enterprise suddenly seemed less likely. My agent told me that the New York publishers were balking at editorial control for the pair, as well they might have. I didn't want to give them control, either, not with my name on it. Frankly, I was relieved and was about to say goodbye to Teko and Yolanda when the as-told-to book morphed into a movie. Tamara Asseyev, who, like most independent producers, was always trying to keep the project alive, had involved one of the major international film directors of that time: Milos Forman.

Dyanne and I met with Milos—he'd just completed *One Flew Over the Cuckoo's Nest*—and any ambivalence we might have felt about collaborating with the Harrises vanished into thin air. We were working with *Milos*, never mind that not one of us, as far as I can recall, had a notion about what the point of view of a movie on this crazy duo might be. (We didn't know quite *how* crazy. It wasn't until Hearst's 1982 autobiography *Every Secret Thing* that it was revealed Emily actually pulled the trigger on the shotgun that killed Myrna Opsahl. The forty-two-year-old woman had the misfortune to be depositing her church collection at a Sacramento bank when the SLA arrived for a hold-up. According to Patty, Emily said of Opsahl's murder "Oh, she's dead, but it doesn't really matter. She was a bourgeois pig anyway.")

With or without a good idea of what we were doing or how we could write a screenplay that everyone would accept, Dyanne and I went with Milos to the LA County Courthouse for a meeting with the Harrises to see what we could come up with. We met Len Weinglass in the lobby. He asked for Forman's official identification to give the LAPD. There was a moment's silence, and then Milos admitted that he didn't have any. The refugee from Communist Czechoslovakia was stateless and without papers. Not only that, the very next day Senator Jacob Javits of New York was putting a special bill before Congress to grant the celebrated director U.S. citizenship.

Weinglass stared at him for a moment and then shook his head. The Chicago 8 lawyer was no stranger to dicey situations and usually relished confrontation, but this was a no-brainer. He told Forman to turn around and get the hell out of there. The last thing the director needed would be the FBI, or somebody, reporting that he'd been consorting with two members of the Symbionese Liberation Army—Patty Hearst's kidnappers, no less—even for filmmaking purposes, the day before his citizenship came up for a vote. He got the picture and took off—and with him, any participation I'd ever have in a movie about Bill and Emily Harris.

My experiences with the Harrises emerged in fictional form in that scene with the Linkers in *The Big Fix* movie. Moses sings "Why Do Fools Fall in Love?," the Frankie Lymon oldie from my New York childhood, with the couple, so that their jailers won't overhear the information being passed back and forth. This again sentimentalizes, and, to a degree, glamorizes, the reality of what happened—something many of us were wont to do in those days. A good number still are. This isn't to say that I regret what I did or wrote. I don't. That was then; this is now. In fact, I'm glad to have participated in many of the events of my time. Those who stood aside missed something worth experiencing, even if in retrospect they would have to admit that this or that cultural event or political trend was nonsense or worse. It may have been, but it was the life of an era, to know it from the inside was and is valuable. Nevertheless, the Harrises *were* really and truly delusional. There is nothing good one can say about them.

One of the more significant and, on balance, positive events of that period was the opening of the People's Republic of China. Nixon made his initial visit in 1972, but few American private citizens had gone themselves as late as 1978, when we were gearing up for the production of *The Big Fix*. I'd been heavily involved in film in one way or another for several years, and it had been a long time since I'd written a Moses Wine novel. I knew that it would be a good time to do another with the movie coming out. Already somewhat bored with the conventional noir/Los Angeles detective genre and becoming more interested in the international thrillers of le Carré and others, I decided to expand the series by taking my hero on one of the tours to China.

Of course, I wouldn't dream of writing this without having gone to China myself. The question was: how to do it? At most one or two trips went per year with very limited spaces. Pat Stitch, an actress friend of mine, had been on one the year before with several notable Hollywood lefties, including Jane Fonda. But there didn't seem to be a repeat coming in the near future and I wasn't sure I was that interested in traveling with a movie crowd, anyway. I did have an interesting connection, however—a man named Richard Hunter who was both an architect and a private detective. He'd developed this unlikely combination of careers through investigations he did for building contractors involved in lawsuits. I used him on occasion as a source for my novels. In fact, he had a kind of Philip Marlowesque quality, a man straight out of the Forties—tall, unflappable, and of few but meaningful words. He was also—and this was the important thing—a lifelong communist or socialist of some more extreme stripe with close ties to the Chinese; he knew Zhou Enlai personally (how was unclear) and had been to the PRC several times.

I told Richard Hunter what I was planning and, after some time and effort, some phone calls back and forth, and veiled talk that I was being "looked into," he arranged for me to join the comically named U.S. China People's Friendship Association's People's Friendship Tour #2. This was a group of about twenty "community and union activists," about as far from a Hollywood crowd as you could go. I flew with them that August to Hong Kong, the participants checking each other out, developing alliances, romantic and otherwise, that would later surface, somewhat disguised, in my novel *Peking Duck*. After a day or so in the quite British Hong Kong, we rode the train to the simple border bridge then separating the New Territories from the People's Republic and negotiated it on foot. Ahead of us was a small, almost ascetic greeting center, a tinny version of "The East Is Red" playing through loudspeakers. It was like crossing into a parallel universe, an Oz of people in blue pajamas.

Although there were hints to the contrary, the PRC was still for the most part in the Maoist era, emerging from the Cultural Revolution and engaged in the rectification campaign against the nefarious "Gang of Four"—including Mao's widow Jiang Qing—who were being blamed for the excesses of that era. Everywhere we went, from that initial humble greeting center to Shanghai's Bund itself, we were confronted by giant billboards (and sometimes even puppet shows) attacking the "Gang" or supporting then Communist Party leader Chairman Hua Guofeng. "Chairman Mao Trusted Chairman Hua Completely," our guides would dutifully translate. "The People and Army Warmly Endorse Him, Too." Who knew if this was true? One had to be somewhat suspicious. But we gringos were a complete rarity in that world, as far out of water as any fish could be. The only other foreigners we encountered on our entire tour were a team of Ethiopian volleyball players who would turn up in locales as disparate as the Great Wall and a sheet metal factory in Manchuria. In fact, it was in Manchuria that we were considered so exotic that several hundred locals—anxious to gape at the white people in garish clothes—followed us in long lines down the streets, pretending they weren't watching when we turned back to smile at them.

My initial reaction to China was one of complete amazement, almost awe. Not only was this my first trip to a communist country; it was also my first trip to Asia. (That latter fact was of tremendous importance. Later I was to visit Cuba and the Soviet Union, where I was at least generally familiar with the cultures—in Cuba, I could even speak the language—and was instantly able to see nuances not available to me in China.) This helped to enhance my "alternative universe" feeling as well as the nagging thought that maybe the Chinese Communists were right—maybe this widely egalitarian world *was* the best way to live.

After all, they seemed to be free of the envy and competition of the

Western world, characteristics which were magnified in the Hollywood environment from which I came. There was an eerie calm about China then, with few automobiles and only the incessant *ching-ching* of bicycle bells interrupting a pre-modern silence. It was crowded, but it wasn't *crowded*. The people were poor, but they weren't *poor*. No one seemed really to be wanting. Everyone had what they called "three rounds and a sound"—a watch, a sewing machine, a bicycle, and a transistor radio. Should any of us want more than that in this materialistic world?

Perhaps I was suffering from a form of Stockholm Syndrome myself in the midst of all this, because I was able to speculate, often positively, on the superiority of their system even though I knew at the time that the Cultural Revolution had been brutal and that I was visiting a country whose perverted logic made Orwell's *Animal Farm* look rational. Part of the reason for this, of course, is that I was *permitted* to visit; I was one of the chosen few. Nearly everybody I knew had been to Paris, but almost no one had been to Peking. And *no one* had been to Manchuria, riding a train, as I did, from Mukden to Dalian, then slipping over the border into North Korea to be entertained with regional dances at a farming commune.

All the time I was in China I thought: Wait until I get home and tell everybody about *this*—in a novel or just on the Hollywood cocktail circuit. And "this"—in whatever form—couldn't be about how bad China was, because what would be the point? It had to be basically positive to create envy and admiration. Still, it couldn't justifiably be a repeat of Lincoln Steffens's famous remark, "I have seen the future and it works!," immediately following the Russian Revolution. That would make no sense. But it could be close enough, the same general idea with appropriate reservations.

Meanwhile, I'd developed a huge crush on one of our guides.

This happened in Shanghai, a city whose very name meant intrigue, romance, and glamour, even under communism. It had been in Shanghai that the "Gang of Four" had developed the ultra-Left strategies that formed the Cultural Revolution just as then, in the late Seventies, it was in that city that the same ideas had been unraveled, that a small number of citizens were wearing not blue pajamas but washed-out pastel floral prints like one could buy at discount houses in the Bronx. As Mrs. Liu, the guide on whom I had a crush, told me, "The proletariat likes bright colors."

Not that the uniformity of the Cultural Revolution didn't have its own attractions. Before arriving in Shanghai, we had stopped at what was known as a May 7th Cadre School. Established by a May 7, 1968 directive from Mao, these rural locations, farms mostly, were places to which intellectuals, teachers, journalists, bureaucrats, and other cultural workers were "sent down," in the parlance of the Great Leap Forward, to perform manual labor and to undergo ideological reeducation—to be "de-classed."

One friendly teacher I talked to had been cleaning pigpens for the better part of a year. She said she enjoyed it, and I believed her. Even now, from a perspective of nearly thirty years, I can see how oddly appealing it was. ("First do the dishes," as the Zen roshis say.) It may be totalitarian in its approach, but the idea that "cultural workers" might learn something from working people is not without merit. Plenty of intellectuals I know today could profit from some "ideological reeducation" through manual labor, but perhaps from a different viewpoint from the one Mao envisioned—and preferably in free-market pigpens.

I guess I was ready for further "reeducation" of a different sort myself when I met Mrs. Liu. Very few times in my life have I been struck so quickly in the heart—struck, needless to say, by the unattainable. Our group, having just arrived in Shanghai, was led into a meeting room in an austere housing project for an introduction to the city by our guide team. South China in August—with no air conditioning, needless to say—was sweltering. There she was, standing at the head of the table, a beautiful young woman with short black hair and piercing black, intelligent eyes. She was most likely in her late twenties, crisp and confident, addressing us, welcoming us to Shanghai. She spoke almost entirely in party rhetoric, talking about the People this, the People that, but I could tell she was brilliant; I was smitten.

She introduced herself as "Mrs. Liu." Was she married, I wondered, or was this just a form of communist politesse, designed to discourage interracial mingling—or mingling of any sort? China then seemed the most prudish, unisex place imaginable, in extreme rebellion against Shanghai's infamous period of ubiquitous prostitution and decadence, attributable, it seemed, to the bourgeoisie, foreigners, and those ever-present "bad elements."

My crush deepened as we traipsed around behind our guides to the usual round of factories, communes, and monuments, including the one-time foreigners-only enclave where there once hung, Mrs. Liu pointed out, the notorious sign "No Chinese and dogs." *I* certainly wasn't feeling that way. I think, in a certain way, Liu realized it. Men are men and women women, whether they communicate via Petrarchan sonnets or "Marxism-Leninism-Mao Tsetung-thought."

Soon enough Liu and I found ourselves walking together through the various destinations, conversing about this and that, the subject matter gradually drifting away from the specific activities of our tour. I remembered discussing Watergate, of all things, with her. She'd never heard of the scandal and was surprised by the disdain in which I held Nixon. (She might be equally surprised at my opinion of him now.) I thought that I was being subversive, demonstrating to a devoted communist—at least she appeared to be one—that it was good to distrust your leaders. After a day or two, I began to ask her about her personal life. She was, indeed, married, but her husband lived thousands of miles away in Szechwan Province where he worked as an engineer. The state assigned them separate roles, so they were only able to see each other a couple of times a year. They had no children. I asked how she felt about this, but she didn't answer.

Our last night in Shanghai we were taken to a concert as a "special treat." I sat beside Liu as an orchestra played Borodin, until recently forbidden music under the strict cultural regime of Madame Mao. My hand brushed against hers, but that is as far as things went. I remember her waving at me tentatively as our group got onto our bus the next day. In my novel *Peking Duck*—a fairly sophisticated knockoff of *Murder on the Orient Express* set in the PRC—Moses Wine sleeps with Mrs. Liu on the night train from Shanghai to Beijing, probably not the first such wish fulfillment in the history of fiction. I didn't even bother to change her name, probably hoping that somehow that she'd read it.

Perhaps she did. Not long after the book was published in the U.S. in 1979, it appeared as *samizdat* in the People's Republic of China. I often wonder what readers over there made of it. It wasn't a completely unsympathetic treatment of the PRC, although, by the time I returned to

Los Angeles, writing and living my normal life, my love affair with the country and the woman had diminished in intensity. I realized what a totalitarian world I'd been visiting. Still, I wanted to preserve my reputation as a cutting-edge radical and liberal and struck a balance in the book that I wouldn't have today. Nevertheless, a screenwriter friend told me at the time that whatever its novelistic strengths and weakness, *Peking Duck* would last as a valuable historical record of what it was like for the first wave of foreigners to visit China in the Seventies. That didn't mean much to me then—I was hoping for higher praise—but looking back I'm pleased to have done that much.

Besides my normal work, for the next year or so after returning from China, I delivered lectures, illustrated with slides I had taken, about the PRC at various venues from a reformed synagogue in Bel Air to a health spa in Tecate, Mexico. I again took what I thought was a balanced attitude, but the net result was undoubtedly more sympathetic than I should have been to a despotism. Of course, the enduring question with China is how to change its system—or whether it is even possible to influence the most populous nation on Earth with its now-gigantic economic motor.

Several months after I left China, I got to shake hands (again through the offices of private detective Richard Hunter) with the man who *did* change China, arguably more significantly and permanently than Mao— Deng Xiaoping. The legendary Chairman of the Communist Party, the man who emerged from prison to do ideological battle with Mao and his followers and to put China on the "capitalist road," was touring the U.S. in the company of the Osmond family. (I kid you not!) I was invited to a small union hall near downtown LA, not far from Richard Hunter's office, for a "friends of China" reception for the Chairman. The entire event was surreal. When I arrived, Chairman Deng and his entourage of perhaps a dozen (all in blue Mao suits), plus about a hundred "friends," watched as the Osmonds danced and sang their plastic, Disneyish numbers. The Chairman, who was well under five feet tall and the shortest person in the room, grinned and clapped along.

When the music was over, he was introduced to us one by one. Most of the "friends" were lefties—radical lawyers, social workers, union leaders—and of a "certain age." I couldn't help but wonder, as they smiled in awe shaking Deng's hand, how many changes in "party line,"

Chinese *and* Soviet, these old rads had endured unquestioningly. Here they nodded in appreciation to a man who, seen from even a few feet off, was clearly intent on steering China as far away from socialism as practicable at that particular moment in history, and wanting to do it as quickly as possible. But he was Chinese and in a Mao suit. It was all very confusing.

In a way, it's even more confusing now. I never would have dreamed that I would be writing these words nearly three decades later on an Apple computer *manufactured* in Shanghai or that I would have been in-volved in a campaign *against* the cooperation of the giant U.S. corpora-tions Google, Yahoo, and Microsoft with the Chinese government. In 2005, I made one of the first online videos for Pajamas Media—the new blog aggregation of which I have become CEO—with the late Congress-man Tom Lantos in protest of the behavior of those Internet behemoths who, in their own self-interest, had allowed the Chinese government to use their services for purposes of anti-democratic censorship and, in the case of Yahoo, worse—the incarceration of a Chinese dissident.

But more surprisingly, and far more personally, Deng Xiaoping helped justify my own very public departure from the Left when I began blog-ging in 2003. I explained my transformation by referencing on several occasions Chairman Deng's well-known words when seeking to wrench China from the self-destructive shackles of communist ideology: "I don't care whether a cat is black or white. I only care if it catches mice." No American pragmatist wrote truer words. They beat all the sayings in Mao's *Little Red Book* put together (except, perhaps, for the sad truth about power coming from the barrel of a gun), and they inspire me to this day. When I think back on that little gnome-like man whose hand I shook years ago, baffled as I was at that time that he was the most pow-erful person in the most populous country on Earth, I have tremendous respect for him—even though I am aware of his ruthlessness. Few politi-cal leaders in history have managed a transformation of the magnitude Deng has. His form of state capitalism—flawed as it is—has brought China into the modern world.

4 DADDY RICH, ABBIE, THE BABY MOGULS, AND MY EARLY BRUSH WITH IDENTITY POLITICS

The first time I met Richard Pryor, he was pretty close to dead drunk. A tumbler of Scotch in his hand, he stumbled into his home office where I had been waiting for some time with Thom Mount and Sean Daniel—two Universal Studio executives—and, after the briefest of introductions, turned to Sean, stared at him for a second, and said, "You don't like me, do you?"

It was a moment of stunning emotional honesty, almost inappropriate, but somehow not; one had the immediate sense that Pryor was telling the absolute truth. Nevertheless, Daniel made a nervous denial, asserting that he liked the comic—who was then (1980) by far Universal's highest-grossing star—very much. Very, very much. Richard wasn't buying it. Apparently, Sean had been on the set as an executive for Pryor's most recent movie, and although the men had barely talked, the highly intuitive comedian could read something he didn't like in the exec's eyes.

This uncomfortable moment was swept under the rug almost as rapidly as it surfaced, but it forever endeared Richard Pryor to me—not that I needed much endearing. I pretty much idolized him at that point, and to some extent still do. He is the only artist I have ever worked with deserving of the epithet "genius" (well, maybe Woody Allen, too, but his genius was of a type that I could understand and was less in awe of—and I didn't work that closely with Woody, anyway). Most of the big movie people I've known, actors and directors, have kissed the derrieres of studio executives. And on rare occasions when they didn't, it was just to lord it over the studio people (now it's my turn, you talentless creep!). Not Richard. For all his greatness and stardom, Richard Pryor treated people high and low alike. He was always honest, as rough on himself as he was on others. It was the secret of his art. And Sean was taking the brunt of it that night.

The purpose of that meeting was to introduce me to Pryor as the screenwriter of his next film, then entitled *Family Dream*. My agent, Sam Adams, had told me a few days before that Thom Mount and Sean Daniel wanted to know if I would like to work with the comedian. I answered in the affirmative in less than the proverbial New York minute. I knew it was one of those rare opportunities to be seized without reservations. *The Big Fix*, which I'd written for Universal, was in the can; for that short period before the film's release, I was the "flavor of the month," as they say in the industry. Into my lap had fallen the chance to work with a man many—myself included—considered the greatest stand-up comedian of all time.

So began the rather amazing saga of the movie ultimately called *Bustin' Loose*, on which I was hired thrice and fired twice, almost directed but didn't, but finally won a prize for writing—a prize I was asked to decline for socio-political reasons. During this time the movie was filmed once, nearly discarded in its entirety, and then shot all over again after a delay of several months. The cause of the delay was Richard Pryor's highly publicized freak accident: He'd nearly burned himself to death smoking a crack pipe. He had to be photographed carefully on that second go-round to hide the scars all over his face and hands. Ironically, all this was for a wholesome film aimed principally at the family audience.

But I get ahead of myself.

That night I drove out to Pryor's estate in Northridge in the San Fernando Valley with Thom Mount and Sean Daniel in Thom's Mustang convertible. Mount is said to be the model for the protagonist of Michael Tolkin's Hollywood novel *The Player*. That may be, but in those days he and Daniel were known as the "Baby Moguls," so branded by *Time* and *New York Magazine* for the extreme youth at which they rose to positions of studio power. At that point, Thom was probably just over thirty and Sean still in his twenties, though they both had been at the top of Universal for several years and had been involved with the making of *Animal House*, among other huge hits.

These young men—like the other famous "baby mogul," Mark Rosenberg, who had been my agent and became an executive at Warner Brothers—were known to be politically left, in Mark's case rather far left. Mount, more traditionally liberal, came from an important Democratic Party family in North Carolina that was close to that state's Senator Sam Ervin, of Watergate fame. Despite having graduated from hippie-centric Bard College and subsequently from the equally bohemian Cal Arts, Thom kept the backslapping affect of a Southern Pol, calling you "killer" and giving you semi-playful punches in the shoulder. The Good Old Boy routine was in his blood. He was the kind of slippery character who charmed your pants off even while you knew he was picking your pocket. He was also the next thing to a congenital liar, to such an extent that you didn't take it seriously or personally.

This strange relationship to the truth, however, could be an asset to him as an executive and producer. Mount was the executive producer of the first film I directed, the late lamented *My Man Adam*—a high school version of *The Secret Life of Walter Mitty*. When we were trying to get the greenlight for the film, a draft of the script had been submitted to the studio, Tri-Star. Tri-Star in those days (1985) decided on greenlighting films via the odd (for Hollywood) system of a majority vote of nine executives. On this first pass, my script narrowly failed five votes to four. Thom, a more experienced and formerly more powerful studio exec than any in the Tri-Star group, buttonholed one of their junior execs and asked her why she had rejected our script. The woman said she was confused by the role of the CIA agent in the screenplay.

"What an idiot," I exclaimed to Mount. As we both knew, there wasn't even a reference to the CIA, let alone an agent, in the screenplay. She probably hadn't even read it. If she had, her comprehension level was embarrassingly low. "What'd you tell her?" I asked Mount, thinking we should set her straight, but Thom was having none of that. "I said you're right," he replied. "We'll change it." With barely a word altered, *My Man Adam* was greenlit on its next draft. It was masterful work by Mount. I told that story for years as "Zen and the Art of the Studio Executive."

Sean was different. The boyish Daniel was a New Yorker and the son of a blacklisted screenwriter who had committed suicide. The first time I met him he couldn't have been more than twenty-two and was trying to get me to write a screenplay about the Weather Underground. I remember the scene fairly well. We were at somebody's treehouse-style hippie abode in Laurel Canyon, a perfect Joni Mitchell "ladies of the canyon" place not far from where I lived.

Daniel pitched me the story. My immediate reaction was that no one would want to make it and that I didn't want to waste my time allying myself with such a project. Besides, who was this twenty-two-year-old kid who thought he could produce a movie? I had no idea that within four years he'd be one of the top three executives at the biggest studio in Hollywood. The difficulty in predicting executive talent is also why there can be those meteoric rises, as with the "baby moguls," especially in an industry where youth is king and the seventeen-year-old boy the most reliable and therefore the most coveted audience.

In those days, the average seventeen-year-old boy was still heavily under the influence of hippie culture, rock and roll, and the whole anti-Vietnam gestalt, so being close to this and having some radical background was a junior executive's ticket to a big studio job. But this didn't mean the "baby moguls" spent much of their time making political movies. Quite the contrary. For the most part, they were the last ones to do it. A Sean Daniel got his liberal-left bona fides by running around at age twenty-two trying to produce a movie about the Weather Underground or as a teenager by, as in his case, being president of high school SDS (the legendary Students for a Democratic Society). By the time he was in the studio system, he'd be spending his time on goofball comedies like *Caddyshack*.

Universal Studios was not in the business of making *The Battle of Algiers*, and he knew it. Even the Vietnam movies of that time and the recent slate of anti-Iraq War films were not really leftist, but just *bien pensant* anti-war flicks. A Hollywood film recommending Vietcong victory or genuine revolution, like Jorge Sanjines's *The Principal Enemy*, would never have been considered by people like Sean or Thom, if you brought them that kind of idea at the studio—although, of course, they would tell you, as a compadre, how great they thought those movies were and wasn't it too bad we couldn't make them. If, like me, you considered yourself a serious, aspiring left-wing filmmaker (more precisely, like me, pretended to yourself that you were one), you wouldn't go to the "baby moguls" with a political project, not usually, anyway. You would go to some square-seeming studio exec who would be more likely to do it because he or she could get credit with the creative community for backing such a project. The "baby moguls" were too afraid for their jobs. Besides, they already had that liberal and leftist credit aplenty. That was the last thing they needed.

I learned this at close range when I became good friends—almost best friends, for a while; he lived at my house during his divorce—with the man who was, superficially, the most leftist and for a time the most successful of all the "baby moguls"—Mark Rosenberg. He was a student lefty from the University of Wisconsin who grew up in the New Jersey suburbs and wanted to be in the movie business. He also acted as if he wanted revolution in America (who knew in what form?) and was brilliant as a young man at making this leftism work for him with the right people.

He probably did have a more legit radical past than most. One time, on a first-class plane ride to New York, he proudly showed me his extensive FBI file, which he had just obtained under the Freedom of Information Act. It went on for pages—they were obviously watching him closely—with many sentences and paragraphs blacked out. Some of those, he alleged, concerned his relationship with the Black Panthers, and the FBI didn't want to jeopardize its sources. Mark told me that he had, among other things, given the Panthers the use of his credit card so they could travel and purchase necessities, including, he implied, weapons. Mark was a master at turning this past to his advantage. Part of the reason for this was his warm, outgoing, almost glad-handing personality. His politics also gave a veneer of do-gooderism to a life that was at heart not so far from that of the fictional Sammy Glick.

As a young man in New York, fresh out of Wisconsin, he developed a close friendship and an alliance of sorts with the young Paula Weinstein. Paula, who would herself become a producer and studio executive at Twentieth Century Fox, was the daughter of Hannah Weinstein, a producer who moved to London during the McCarthy period and was among the only ones to employ blacklisted writers.

Hannah had formed an ex-pat community of sorts in the UK. This made her famous on the Hollywood Left, so in a sense the Weinsteins, mother and daughter, were a royal family with deep roots and many connections into the past. (I attended Hannah's memorial service in 1984. It was held in a private room at the Beverly Wilshire and was attended by, among other luminaries of the literary and cinematic Left, playwright Lillian Hellman. Swathed in a luxurious mink coat in Southern California, she entered in a wheelchair with—I am not joking—the labor anthem "I Dreamed I Saw Joe Hill Last Night" discreetly playing, naturally in the famous Paul Robeson rendition, as memorial background music over the five-star hotel's loudspeaker. Even then I thought: this is black comedy!)

Mark came to Hollywood with these impressive liberal-left contacts and soon enough landed an agency job with Adams, Ray & Rosenberg (not a relation). He was aggressive at wooing new clients, using the political soul-brother connection to whatever degree was necessary. He used it extensively on me, of course mixing it with the usual "I can make you a great writer-director" line, stealing me for Adams, Ray & Rosenberg from my first movie agency William Morris. It wasn't long after that, however, that Mark left the agency business and became a Warner Brothers executive. At that point he had never made a deal for me as an agent, but having a friend inside the studio promised good things. We could exploit the system to make revolutionary films.

As it turned out, the revolution would have to wait. Mark Rosenberg, like the other "baby moguls," made few, if any, genuinely left-wing films. In fact, once ensconced in their positions, they were the antithesis of left-wing, riding around in studio Mercedes and going to fancy expense-account dinners. Through Mark, however, I did experience one odd exception to the "no *real* left-wing movie rule," on the part of the "baby moguls," but it wasn't because of him. Someone else requested me and he was the conduit. In 1979, just before I was supposed to leave for Cuba to attend the first festival of the New Latin American Cinema—an event Mark was also supposed to attend but ultimately bypassed for "business reasons"—I received a phone call from him. Jay Presson Allen—the screenwriter of *The Prime of Miss Jean Brodie*, *Cabaret*, and other films, now turned producer with a deal at Warner Brothers—had seen *The Big Fix* and wanted me to write a film for her to produce. The movie would be based on the life of Bertell Ollman, an eccentric NYU politics professor who'd invented a Marxist version of Monopoly called "Class Struggle." Ollman was actually trying to promote the game in the normal manner—flogging it at toy business conventions and so on—in order to teach people, well... the class struggle.

The professor had written an amusing op-ed for the *New York Times* about his experiences as a Marxist businessman. This piece had caught Jay's eye and the writer/producer had optioned Ollman's life story. Mark said he and Allen agreed I was the only one they could think of with sufficient left-wing background and sense of irony to pull this off as a commercial film. Although I had my doubts, I was flattered and figured: why not?

Upon my return from Cuba, I started working on the script with Jay, hanging out at her tony estate in Litchfield County, Connecticut, and meeting her even tonier neighbors William Styron and Philip Roth. By the end, we had produced what we both thought was a rather wry screenplay called "Class Struggle" in the tradition of the Italian comedies of Pietro Germi and Lina Wertmüller. Although the script was sympathetic enough to the somewhat goofy but idealistic professor's ups and downs in the world of business, it wasn't overtly political, trying instead to make fun of the collision of capitalist and socialist cultures. (When he read it, Ollman was angry with me for betraying the revolution.) Still, it was far from your average Warner Brothers movie in tone and subject matter.

Mark Rosenberg was enthusiastic when he read the draft. "I knew you could do it!" he exclaimed. "This is an absolute go picture!" I was still young enough to believe him. Within a week or so, the real word came back from the studio. The script was not what they had "expected." What had they expected? A love story between a bumbling downtown professor and a glamorous Park Avenue debutante was suggested. Did we really need this *Marxist* Monopoly game? He could be a geology professor. The political material was unnecessary and would just "confuse" the audience.

Mark delivered this news to me in a matter-of-fact manner with no mention at all of our previous conversation, assuming that naturally I'd cooperate in the evisceration of my own work. I didn't. I passed on it, not so much for idealistic reasons but because I knew I could never write the movie they had in mind to anybody's satisfaction, assuming they had anything in mind, really. But this only underscored what I suspected then and now know. The politics of the "baby moguls" was not to be taken seriously. It was more of a pose than a real view or commitment, and continues to be so to this day. What they really wanted was to be rich and powerful. Everything else—including and especially the politics—was a means to that end or, more precisely, an excuse for it.

Pryor understood all this better than anyone. He had lived in Berkeley and knew the scene intimately, would make fun of it when we sat together working on the script for what was then called *Family Dream*. But the hypocrisy of all this pseudo-leftism didn't bother him. It just amused him. It didn't bother me much in those days, either. I was profiting from it.

But I never would have predicted one of the most bizarre events that happened in my life during those days of the Baby Moguls—and it occurred while I was beginning work on the script for Richard. I had been using his bungalow on the Universal lot to write the screenplay, since the comedian almost always preferred to stay at his mansion in Northridge. The bungalow had several rooms, which I basically had to myself (I also had a secretary who came in and out); I was right next door to the Cheech and Chong bungalow, center of a fair amount of the behavior you would expect from the stars of *Up in Smoke*. I was always too hard working—puritan, really—to participate in much of that, especially during the day, so the major perk of writing at the studio for me was the free use of the screening rooms. A writer or producer could simply call a studio number and order up a film for "research" purposes, a delicious privilege in that pre-videocassette and -DVD era.

One day I decided, thanks to a desire both to procrastinate and to fill a gap in my film history knowledge, to request a viewing of *To Be or Not to Be*, Ernst Lubitsch's classic comedy about disguise. As it happened, the subject couldn't have been more appropriate. I was alone in the screening room, watching the movie, sitting in the back row to be near the telephone if the movie was boring—it was anything but, in this case—when the door cracked open. I peered through the darkness as a man slipped into the room followed by a woman and a child. I could only see them in silhouette when the man spoke to me in a stage whisper: "Roger?"

I strained for a look as the man drew closer, his Harpo Marx-like hair outlined against the black and white movie screen like a costumed character out of the Lubitsch film. The surreal image could only be one person, at least only one person I knew. "Abbie?" I whispered, wondering if I sounded as incredulous as I felt.

Abbie Hoffman nodded. I looked from him to the woman and child who were still by the theater door. I assumed that they were his wife Anita and son america (with a lowercase "a"). Or it could have been that other woman Johanna he was rumored to be with. I didn't know. In any case, what was he doing there? He was supposed to be underground then, probably on the Ten Most Wanted list at that very moment. "It's amazing to see you here," I said.

He took a couple of steps forward. "I saw your movie," he said coldly. Apparently this was not a friendly visit. I didn't know the man well, having only met him once at a party years before, and looked at him apprehensively. "Why'd you do that to me?" he asked.

"Do what?" I asked, but almost immediately I understood. The movie version of *The Big Fix* had been in theaters three weeks or so and he must have seen it. Or heard about it, anyway. An important part of the story centered on a search for a character from the Sixties, Howard Eppis, who had gone underground. In the movie (as opposed to in the book), you got to meet Eppis "hiding in plain sight," as the saying from mystery novels goes. The former revolutionary lived a very comfortable bourgeois lifestyle—thank you very much—under a new name as a successful advertising man in the San Fernando Valley. "If you can write 'Ho, Ho, Ho Chi Minh/ Viet Cong is gonna win," Eppis tells Moses Wine, while flipping burgers at his poolside barbecue, "you can write Coke commercials!" I meant it as satire, of course, but Abbie must have taken it as a personal insult, especially since some reviewers had identified Hoffman, the indefatigable Chicago 8 defendant, with Eppis, the sell-out.

I don't remember precisely what Abbie said after that, but it ended up with my apologizing guiltily (for no reason, really) and asking him not to take what I did seriously. It was a movie, after all, and Eppis was a composite character, more Jerry Rubin than Abbie, anyway. All this happened in a minute or two before Hoffman, somewhat mollified, told me he had to go. He had an appointment elsewhere in the studio. On his way out, I asked him what it was that brought him to Universal anyway, risking apprehension. He was there, he said, to sell the film rights to *Steal This Book*. He had a meeting with Thom Mount and Sean Daniel.

Writing this today makes me smile at the absurdity of it all, but I probably took Abbie quite seriously then, given the temper of the times, and there was in all probability such a meeting, although it is unlikely that anything came of it. Universal Studios never made a film version of *Steal This Book*. The legal department no doubt would have looked askance on making a deal with a man in flight from cocaine charges—among other things. Thom and Sean were probably just having fun entertaining Underground Abbie, adding another story for their memoirs and giving me one in the bargain. None of us would have wanted to predict Hoffman's sad ending, dead less than a decade later at age fifty-two with the cause—suicide or accidental overdose—still undetermined.

The movie I was working on with Richard Pryor was, however, being taken seriously by the studio. After that first visit with Mount and Daniel, I had arranged to go out to Pryor's place to meet with the comedian myself. The house was a large California Spanish on a few acres with a boxing ring in back and a miniature Shetland pony running free around the property. Its location in Northridge, far from the traditional Hollywood bailiwicks of Beverly Hills, Brentwood, and Malibu, was itself indicative of something different about Richard. He didn't want to be one of them.

Before I went, I reread the ten-page treatment for *Family Dream*, which had supposedly been written by Pryor, although I'd heard rumblings that someone else had suggested the idea. I was to ignore that, I was told. I didn't need to be. I was already baptized in the cruel world of the movie business. What I really feared was that the film would not be much more than the story I was given, the sentimental tale of an ex-con (Pryor) whose parole officer forces him to drive a group of orphaned children across the country on a bus. Along the way, the ex-con, of course, is humanized by the kids and wins the heart of the children's tart schoolteacher who, also predictably, had been disdainful of the ex-con at the outset. Verna Fields—the former editor of *American Graffiti* and *Jaws* and studio executive in charge of the project, as she had been with *The Big Fix*—summed up the premise well as "*African Queen* on a bus." Only I was afraid this version of *African Queen* would be trite and simplistic.

But I was apprehensive about more than that when I pulled up at Pryor's manse that first time at the appointed hour. What would happen when I had my first face-to-face one-on-one meeting with Richard Pryor? Would I be dismissed as instinctively and peremptorily as Sean

Daniel? The housekeeper, a stout black woman, met me at the door and ushered me inside. "I'm sorry. Mr. Pryor's asleep," she explained, guiding me away from the office, where I had been the first time, and toward the kitchen. "Would you like something to eat? We've got some leftover quiche."

Asleep? It was about two in the afternoon, as I recall. Had Pryor been up that late the night before? I sat down at the kitchen table and ate some quiche. About a half hour after finishing I inquired and was told he was still asleep. An hour later ... still asleep. Perhaps it would be better if I came back another time, the housekeeper said. I came back another time—two days later—but Mr. Pryor was again asleep. It didn't take a detective writer to realize something was going on here.

I called Thom Mount to find out what was up. He said he'd get back to me. A day or so later, Pryor called me himself at the office. He sounded sheepish and apologetic on the phone, said he wasn't feeling well and couldn't work, that I should come out the next day. I did. This time I was ushered straight up to his office. I didn't know what to expect, but I was almost certain at that point the Mr. Pryor had not been "asleep." Given his reputation, he was probably loaded on drugs. But he seemed to be sober that day and we sat down to work as if nothing had happened.

So began my relationship with Richard Pryor, which, at first, couldn't have been better. I would write twenty or so pages of the script, send them to him via a studio courier (this was in the days before email), and then drive out to his place a few days later to discuss them. Pryor was always highly supportive of what I was doing, amazingly so for a movie star. I met the people around Richard, his entourage. It was quite a crew, including his then live-in girlfriend Jennifer Lee, the daughter of the president of Bennington College, whom he would marry and divorce the following year and then remarry (for his seventh marriage) in 2001 when he was suffering from multiple sclerosis; his talented daughter Rain Pryor, on her way to being a stand-up comic herself; his somewhat hapless son Richard Junior; his trainer Rashon, who worked out Richard in the boxing ring, and his dealer "The Rev" who would turn up every few days in a Rolls Royce with immense quantities of cocaine.

I came face to face with the Rev's bounty before I met the man himself, when I walked into Pryor's office one day to be confronted by a solid brick of the white powder sitting on the comedian's desk. Richard himself was sitting behind it, studying me as I tried not to gape at the brick. I had never seen a remotely similar quantity of the drug in my life. I couldn't even have begun to compute its street value. "Want some?" he asked, gesturing to a razor blade. "Sure," I said, sensing he was testing me. Richard scraped off a bit of cocaine on a sheet of paper and passed it over to me with the blade. I arranged a line and Pryor watched as I snorted it. From the look on his face, I had the feeling I had passed the test. That was the first and last drug I would ever do with Richard Pryor.

Later, he told me he was relieved I had done it. He was afraid that I was judging him. (That was part of the reason he was always "asleep.") Nothing, as it happened, could have been further from the truth. I had only admiration for Richard Pryor and sympathy for his drug problem.

Only the week before, we had gone together on a research trip for *Family Dream*, driving across the San Fernando Valley in his red convertible Mercedes coupe to an orphanage in Sunland about an hour away. We were going to meet the orphans for script inspiration. Along the way, when stopped at red lights, almost everyone would recognize Pryor and wave to him. He was a huge celebrity in 1980. If the fans were black, they acted as if they had seen God himself. "Daddy Rich! Daddy Rich!" they called out, referring to the character Pryor played in *Car Wash*, a loveable charlatan in a white fur coat who preached the gospel of money. "We love you, Daddy Rich!"

At the orphanage, the response was similar. Pryor was remarkably kind and gentle with the kids who gathered idolatrously around him. He seemed to empathize with them in a deep way. I wasn't surprised, since I knew a fair amount of his background from our discussions. Richard's mother was a whore and his father a pimp who ran a cathouse in Illinois. Richard had described to me his father holding him up as a young child to the keyhole to watch his mother turn a trick. "How did you react?" I asked, unable even to envision the feelings. "I saw a rose exploding in front of my eye," said Pryor. "It blocked my vision."

I always think of Richard as one of the purest example of genius without formal education. Almost everything came to him by instinct and street learning. In fact, somewhere around our trip to the orphanage I discovered that he wasn't fully literate. I got my first hint of this when he told me of his excitement on discovering I'd also written the novel of *The Big Fix*, before writing the movie. He hadn't known that I wrote something other than screenplays until his girlfriend Jennifer mentioned it from reading the review of the movie version in *Variety*. "You actually wrote a book," he said, shaking his head in near disbelief. This impressed him out of all proportion to reality, at least to the reality I knew. But I started to reflect on why, unlike everyone else I worked with in the movie business, he had given me no detailed script notes. We did all of our work out loud: I told him what I was doing and he reacted verbally. He never referred to the text.

Despite has brilliance, however, Pryor was ashamed of his literacy deficit and wanted to improve his mastery of the written word. Much like a reporter, he kept a small notebook in his pocket and, if someone he trusted used a word he didn't know, he took out the notebook and asked for the spelling, dutifully recording it for future memorization. He didn't take this book out with me at first, but after a while he did, and I always felt awkward spelling out words for him. (Perhaps he shouldn't have trusted me, because I took this habit, which I found touching, and used it in my novel *The Straight Man*, which has a character, the comedian Otis King, based very closely on Richard.)

Once I realized the literacy problem, I started reading the script aloud to Richard deliberately, not a bad strategy in any case, since screenplays are meant to be spoken and photographed and directors often have table readings of scripts before preparing the shooting draft. (Paul Mazursky and I read portions to each other all the time when we were collaborating.) This was a much better way with Pryor, naturally, and we soon had a screenplay with which both of us were happy.

To put on the finishing touches, I accompanied Richard to Detroit where he was doing his one-man show. The audience was almost entirely African–American. His routine then consisted of remarkably granular impersonations of white and black people, how they thought, how they talked, how they walked, down to tiny details like how they wrinkled their noses. He had body control similar to Keaton and Chaplin and could turn himself into another person in front of your eyes, even someone of another race. And he was able to do these impressions totally devoid of racism. Not for one minute did I find Richard racist in the way he performed his act or, for that matter, in the way he treated me or treated others. It almost seemed as if he had seen too much of humanity's failings to be racist. All were mocked and all were forgiven.

But this, of course, was not true of the world around him. I didn't realize it at the time, but the moment we turned the first draft of *Family Dream* into Universal, I was about to become a very small pawn in the continuing collision between racial politics and the entertainment industry. *Family Dream*, it should be noted, was to be one of the first African-American-produced movies in major studio history and the screenwriter, through no fault of his own, happened to be Caucasian.

Exacerbating this situation, although I didn't realize it yet, was my close relationship and growing friendship with Richard, which was becoming a springboard for my own ambitions to be a filmmaker. While we were working on the script, we speculated, as do almost all screenwriters and producers during the writing process, on who might play the other roles and who would direct. From the outset, Richard was focused on Cicely Tyson for the female lead, but on the issue of director, one day he said to me, "You should direct this movie. You understand it better than anybody." At that point I had never directed film, only a small amount of theater, but I certainly wanted to do so. Even so, I acted properly reluctant, though I imagine it was easy to see I was just being polite, especially for someone as instinctive as Pryor. A few days later he repeated that I was the right one to direct the movie, but this time as if it were a fait accompli that I would do it. I asked him if he was sure and he said yes. I was suddenly very excited and extremely nervous. To go from screenwriter with one produced credit to the director of the biggest comic star in the business in one step would be quite a leap indeed. Still, I was more than willing to give it a shot. After all, I thought, I may never again get a chance like this.

So it was against this background that the first draft of *Family Dream* was submitted to Universal. When Thom Mount called to say that they liked it, although they had, as always, some suggestions, Richard informed them that I would direct. He was the producer, after all. More than that, he was a movie star—someone with far more clout than a normal producer and, Mount knew, more than almost any studio executive as well. Movie stars opened movies. If they didn't like the way they were being treated by one studio, which they regarded pretty much as a bank, they could go to another.

I was sitting in Pryor's office when this exchange occurred and was able to see the smile on his face during his conversation with Thom. Richard was not immune to the pleasures of using his power and when he hung up, he told me that Mount was a little surprised, but would have to accept the decision. I should go back to my office at the studio and wait to hear from him. I did, but he didn't call. Several days later, my agent called. The studio was not happy. They felt that my directing was being imposed on them. I called Richard. Richard was unhappy with the studio. He called Thom. Finally, Thom called me—I *would* direct the movie. I should go back to my office and start making my director's plans, do scene sketches, starting thinking about a crew. I did, but I suspected that another shoe would drop. I was right. I was informed a few days later that a new player was involved with this movie—the NAACP. The National Association for the Advancement of Colored People had been putting pressure on Universal Studios to use more black directors and this film seemed like an obvious choice. I was out, my agent told me. Don't even try to fight it, he advised—not that I would have anyway. Who was I to do battle with the NAACP?

Several weeks later I heard that an African-American director named Oz Scott had been selected to direct *Family Dream*. He had never directed a movie before, either, but he'd directed the Broadway production of Ntozake Shange's *For Colored Girls Who Have Considered Suicide When the Rainbow Is Enuf*. I was sad not to be doing it myself, but I was optimistic. Although I hadn't seen it, the play, which had won the Tony, was supposed to be good.

I went to meet with Scott, who now had an office next to mine. We didn't spend much time together. He didn't seem particularly pleased to see me and it was hard to tell what he thought of my script. He had no notes, virtually unheard of for a director. I should have read the writing on the proverbial wall. Next thing I knew, I was fired. An African-American writer was hired, whose name now escapes me, to rewrite me. Such was life in Hollywood—with or without the NAACP. It was hard to blame race politics for this *exclusively*; hiring and firing writers in the movie business was a more common occurrence than getting an oil change for your car. Sometimes they even came back to you. That was what happened in this case, because about two months later I was rehired to work on a new version of the script with Scott. The rewrite he'd turned in had been useless. At this juncture, my friend Richard was nowhere to be seen. Poor Oz Scott, way out of his depth, was soldiering on by himself. I was told to go back to my original screenplay and work with the leading lady, Cicely Tyson.

I naturally respected Cicely—the star of *Sounder* and other films—as an actress. But she had a reputation for being arrogant and rude to the crew and other lesser mortals and I could see why the moment I met her. The first thing she asked me was why she didn't have any funny lines in the screenplay, when Pryor did. Her voice implied that this was some kind of conspiracy on my part; I had a suspicion that nothing I could do would please her. I was right. (And I'd given the funny lines to Pryor because, unlike Cicely, he was funny.) Soon enough I was fired again and the screenwriter of *Sounder*, Lonne Elder III, brought onto the project. After a few months, I read in *Variety* that the movie was being shot in Seattle, but didn't think much about it. I would, at best, share credit on the screenplay, which undoubtedly had been changed beyond recognition. I washed my hands of the whole thing.

But my connection to the movie wasn't over. Verna Fields had been informing me of the progress of the editing process, and it wasn't good. The movie wasn't cutting together. Evidently, Oz Scott didn't have a sense of film continuity. The studio had a lot of money invested in Pryor, but they had a useless film. They were considering doing the unthinkable— starting over, almost from scratch. Oz was fired and Michael Schultz— the director of *Car Wash* and the Negro Ensemble Company—took over. (I never understood why they didn't use Michael in the first place, since he had worked with Richard before and was a vastly more experienced director.)

Verna showed Schultz my original screenplay. He was stunned that they hadn't used that in the first place. Well, "stunned" is probably an exaggeration. No one is "stunned" by good work being passed over in the movie business. But, in any case, I was hired again on the project; I'd now been hired thrice and fired twice. That would be the final count. Michael Schulz and I took what amounted to a few minutes of Oz Scott's existing footage, fashioned a brand new script (using some of my old pages) for the rest, and shot another seven weeks. In essence, the film was shot twice. I was awarded sole screenplay credit by the Writers Guild from a story by Pryor with an adaptation credit for Lonne Elder. The Universal marketing department titled the final movie *Bustin' Loose* and it came out in May 1981 with a poster showing a terrified Richard fleeing from the Ku Klux Klan. It became one of the big hits of that year, remaining the top-grossing movie in the country for about six weeks. It's still a staple on the late show worldwide.

Happy Hollywood ending?

Well, not quite. I happened to be on the East Coast for the New York opening of the movie, which, for reasons unknown to me, I hadn't been told about. Nevertheless, I went over to the theater where it was playing and talked my way in. Up on stage, the "filmmakers" were being presented. Pryor—who rarely came to such events—was not there, but the producers, most of whom had not even been on the set, and some of the actors, were. They were introduced one by one to the tumultuous applause of a mostly black crowd. No one mentioned the writer—any writer. But this was just a preview of what was to come. Back in LA, I got a phone call from the studio telling me that the film was being honored at the first Image Awards, a new award created by the NAACP to celebrate quality films by and about African-Americans. I was being touted for the screenplay prize. Then I heard that no such prize was given. The film was given Best Picture, but it evidently had no writer. I was never invited to the awards ceremony. I was a white non-person.

I was disturbed by this, of course, but I don't remember feeling all that bad. The finished film embarrassed me to a small degree—especially compared to the earlier drafts that were never shot—and I didn't feel like picking up an award for it. I was also enough of a guilty white liberal-cum-ex-civil rights worker in those days not to relish the prospect of winning a prize that was obviously designed for an African-American and should have gone to one. Still, identity politics had reared its ugly head for the first time in my conscious mind. I wasn't being rewarded for my work because of the color of my skin—and I was white. How odd, especially given my history.

It was a confusing state of affairs made more irritating early the next year when, one morning, I opened the *New York Times* business section to read an interview with Sidney Sheinberg, then president of MCA/

Universal. It had been an especially bad year for Universal Pictures, Shei- nberg told the *Times*. Only *Four Seasons* and *Bustin' Loose* had saved the studio from disaster. *Wow*, I thought, visions of moneybags dancing in my head. As sole screenwriter, I had five percent of the producer's net. I quickly called my lawyer. But he just started to laugh. Hadn't I seen my statement? The only person who had a chance of seeing any money out of this was Richard Pryor. He had gross participation. Sure enough, that very day, my statement arrived, showing the movie twelve million dol- lars in the red.

As for that same Richard Pryor who was making out like a bandit because of those gross receipts, I never saw him again. Friends did tell me, from time to time, when they'd run into him at a party, that he sent his best. I have no idea whether he was aware that when the Guild was deciding on credits, Thom Mount called me on his behalf, asking that I not try to share the film's "story by" credit with Pryor, because Richard "loves you and wants to work with you again." I was too naïve at the time to realize that what seemed to me a relatively minor credit (com- pared to the vaunted "screenplay," which I had) was the basis for televi- sion series rights. *Bustin' Loose* was subsequently made into a TV series from which I received not a penny.

True, Pryor didn't behave particularly well toward me at the end, but considering what happened to him, it's hard to stay angry. In 1991 Pryor was diagnosed with multiple sclerosis. It ended his movie career and forced him to curtail and eventually suspend his magnificent stand-up comedy shows. It also made him give up his drug use; he famously said, "God gave me this M. S. shit to save my life." It didn't, ultimately. He died in 2005 from the nervous system disease.

I feel odd writing this story of Pryor now, during the rise of Barack Obama and a whole new era in American race politics. Many views I and others held in those days seem to have outlived their usefulness, though they live on with little examination. Multicultural America is already a reality, but some act as if it's not. And yet I write even those bland words with trepidation. Although once a civil rights worker, I am afraid of be- ing accused of racism.

Back then, in the era of the "baby moguls," it was different. I look at that time as a transitional phase in the development of today's Holly- wood, where conventional liberal-left politics have become the accepted norm, a ticket to employment or, if not that, a safety net for those already employed. Before the "baby moguls," most of the executive class adhered to the traditional Sam Goldwyn view: "If you want to send a message, use Western Union." It was largely the writers who were on the Left in the early days of the industry. Now the Left zeitgeist is pervasive throughout the industry, the same views carrying all the way to the head of the studio. What once was a conventional political decision based on factual analysis or even social class has become much closer to an act of faith than of reason. Inadvertently, the "baby moguls" like Thom Mount and Sean Daniel paved the way for this. They brought the campus atmosphere of the Sixties into the boardrooms of Hollywood. People like me were their less powerful allies.

Mark Rosenberg, that "baby mogul" to whom I was closet, died tragically in 1992 in a freak accident while on location in Texas. At the age of forty-two, he choked to death on some food on the set. A memorial was held for him in the Writers Guild Theatre just a few blocks away from the Beverly Wilshire where I had attended a similar event for Hannah Weinstein. I don't recall "Joe Hill" being played at Mark's as it had been at Hannah's, but Mark's memorial was surely a bigger deal with greater attendance. He was on a trajectory to be studio head somewhere someday and had many friends and business acquaintances that filled the 540-seat theater, its screen dominated by a giant photograph of Mark, an obese man with smiling eyes and bushy-bearded face.

I was forced to stand way at the back to watch. Though it was ostensibly a memorial service for a young movie mogul, the event was dominated by politics with little mention of the art or commerce of film. His old friends from his radical college days were keynote speakers, and they spoke only of his social and political values, although they too had minor screenwriting careers due almost exclusively to Mark's patronage. The grieving widow, Mark's third wife, was now his near-childhood friend Paula Weinstein, daughter of Hannah. A few years before, he and Paula had finally married and formed their own production company, cementing left-wing bloodlines back to the blacklist while living out a posh Hollywood lifestyle with a ranch in Montana and an estate in Brentwood with his and hers Mercedes in the garage.

On the way out of the event I watched as the studio executives and producers gathered together in clutches on the sidewalk outside the theater, shaking hands and nodding their heads. For a moment, I flashed on the funeral scenes in *The Godfather* movies, the competing Dons bowing to Don Corleone. Then I remembered Mark passing my son Raphael, then in his early teens, his first marijuana cigarette while we sat having dinner on the patio of the house Renee and I rented in Coldwater Canyon. It had been a show of machismo, exploiting the unequal power relationship between executives and writers, and I had said nothing, though I felt sick to my stomach. I felt the same way, standing there on the sidewalk that day. Alienation was setting in. *La nausée.* I couldn't see it then, but Los Angeles as I knew it was changing and with it my view of the world.

In just over two years, Nicole Brown Simpson and Ron Goldman would be murdered in Brentwood.

5 THE 1980s VINTAGE

I don't blame Hollywood for the fact that my marriage flew apart in the Eighties. But I do know that Hollywood had something to do with it—and not just because I left my wife for another woman higher in the Industry food chain. Dyanne was yet to make it as a writer and the other woman, Renee Missel, was then a successful producer on the Universal lot where I was working. There were many extenuating circumstances, some of which, to be fair to all concerned, belong in a novel under the mask of fiction and not in a memoir with all names named. Still, what Hollywood had to do with it was more zeitgeist than hierarchy. We were all in a world that distorted and magnified the values of the time—from leftover women's liberation to leftover flower power—through the lens of Hollywood materialism.

And materialism was the order of the day. It was the 1980s, politics and social commitment disappearing almost completely against the inexorable pull of self-interest—like one long line of cocaine up a giant nose. Of course, I knew all this—it wasn't subtle—and tried to shield myself from it by continuing to write my books. It wasn't easy. The distractions were many. But it was during one such an attempt that my marriage finally disintegrated.

In fact, it had been disintegrating for some time. Dyanne said she no longer loved me—later she said that I had taken that too literally—and we both went spiraling off in opposite directions into therapy, Dyanne with a Jungian and I with a Gestalt therapist who dabbled in Zen. It was all very California, very Esalen, although it's sometimes too simple to categorize things that way. Zen Buddhism clearly has its uses. In fact, it might be one of the great enduring practical philosophies by which to live life—if only I had the self-discipline to follow it. And, if I knew more about it, I might find some value in Jungian psychology, too, even though its creator's alleged anti-Semitism is a tough hump for me to overcome. The frequent citation of Jung's work by theoreticians of National Socialism will probably keep me away forever.

In any case, in the midst of all this therapy, which included, for me, Zen sitting and biofeedback sessions, and despite the allures of Hollywood, I decided to write another Wine book. The subject would be Jewish fundamentalism, the location, Israel. I'd been inspired by the wedding of a distant Orthodox relative of Dyanne's. The bride's eighteen-year old brother—an extraordinarily handsome kid with a face off a tourist poster—had returned from Israel for his sister's nuptials. He'd arrived late from the plane and marched in during the reception, wearing a t-shirt and jeans, with a knitted yarmulke on his curly black hair. Instead of toasting his sister, he stood up in front of the large crowd, most of whom were very proper-looking bourgeois Jews, thrust his fist in the air in a Jewish imitation of the Black Power salute, and shouted out to all that Greater Israel belonged to the Jews and he was prepared to die for Hashem—the popular name for God in Hebrew. He stared out at the audience with a kind of challenge, as if he alone were living an authentic life. It was an electrifying moment of a certain sort. I later saw photos of the youth in Israel with an Uzi on his back, out on patrol for the Jewish Defense League. He was a member and a follower of their militant leader, the controversial Rabbi Meir Kahane of Brooklyn, then of Jerusalem.

At that very moment, I decided to write about a book about the fanatics of the JDL, the kind of Jew whom I could never be, yet who still fascinated me. I took as my inciting incident a recent bombing of a militant Arab in Orange County that was blamed on the Jewish Defense League. I'd put Moses Wine in the middle of it, a Jewish detective hired by the Arabs to investigate the Jews. And I'd send him to Israel, where he'd never been, to solve the crime.

I'd never been there either, and this would give me a good excuse to go. I was arranging my trip when Dyanne's parents heard about it and wanted their daughter to go, too. They even offered to pay for her part of the trip. What they didn't know was the state of our marriage. Actually, the two weeks we spent together in Israel was a kind of interregnum during which our relationship was reasonably calm, but then I left to return to the States by myself, ostensibly to begin my book, while

Dyanne stayed abroad. What I began instead was an affair with another woman while my wife was in Switzerland having therapy sessions with two Jungian shrinks.

I was guilty as hell when she came back and immediately confessed the affair with the other woman, whereupon Dyanne confessed that *she* had been having an affair with one of my oldest friends. It was rather like the screenplay for *Scenes from a Mall* that I wrote years later, but unlike the two characters in the movie, we did not reconcile after our admissions. We split apart and I eventually married Renee Missel, the woman with whom I'd been having the affair. This was accompanied by plenty of *sturm und drang* for all concerned—there were kids involved on our side—and it was certainly the most difficult part of my life.

That the novel didn't get written was the least of it. Indeed, I had no choice but to throw myself into Hollywood for financial reasons, to support the high cost of marital dissolution. That was ironic, because Hollywood was in some small way the cause of our divorce, but only to whatever degree that we aren't responsible for our own lives and are creatures of our environment. Dyanne and I were the kind of writers who reviled the movie industry but still clung to it for status and economic succor—a form of bad faith that made marriage difficult. Even more difficult is that we married too young in an era when people were living jazz and kicks.

So the Eighties for me were years of emotional turmoil mixed with careerism. Everything was about the self. Liberal politics, while still there as a form of image or definition, were in the background. It was also the era of those Hollywood favorites cocaine and ecstasy, both of which I indulged in with some frequency. I was trying to make up for lost time in the realm of experience, but I was doing it in tandem with my new significant other Renee, who wanted the security of marriage shortly after we started living together. (She had her reasons. She was a French Canadian from a broken home, her mother the erratic lover of the novelist Antoine de Saint Exupéry and the separatist leader René Levesque when Renee was a child of three or four.) This was obviously contradictory to a bohemian lifestyle, but I was in such emotional disarray, so insecure myself, I didn't know how to stop it.

Besides, I found Renee glamorous. She had connections to the upper echelons of Hollywood, famous directors and studio executives, and had a personality that was attractive to these kinds of people. She knew how to deal with them in ways I never could. I was riding along on her coattails, or skirttails, as it were. But I knew something was wrong. By the time we were getting married, I was certain that we had done the wrong thing, but I didn't have the courage to stop it. On our wedding day I picked up a paperback of *The Name of the Rose* and lost myself in Umberto Eco for most of our Tahiti honeymoon, reading the novel standing up in the bathroom while Renee slept. The marriage was over before it started.

Still, Renee was a vibrant and exciting person and she opened up a lot of doors for me—even if some of them might have been better off staying shut. One of those doors led to the screenwriter, soon to be director, Oliver Stone. Oliver and Renee had been a duo at the time he won his first Oscar for writing *Midnight Express*. Renee described him rolling around the floor of the limousine, clutching the statue in glee. I doubt that was much of an exaggeration. When I first visited him at his house, he took me into his office to show me his Oscar, which was illuminated by a special spotlight lest you fail to notice it.

Oliver and I didn't get along well. From the start there was a competitive underpinning to our relationship, a fair amount of it, I admit, coming from my envy of his burgeoning reputation as Hollywood's premier political filmmaker. That didn't stop me from thinking that *Salvador*—his first and, to my mind, best, directorial effort—was a powerful and original film. Whatever one feels about the extremists on both sides of the Salvadoran civil war, the film works as a populist document with great sympathy for the Salvadoran people. The cast is good. James Woods—who later became something of a Hollywood apostate himself—does a fine job as the Hunter S. Thompsonish gonzo journalist hero. And Oliver demonstrated great filmmaking skills from the outset; he was better as a director than he ever was as a writer.

But even then a kind of paranoia lurked close to the surface, a paranoia that would later express itself overtly in the delusional scenes of *JFK*, in which the filmmaker seemed to be advocating the most dubious of conspiracy theories regarding Kennedy's assassination. And even though I opposed the Vietnam War, I found his Vietnam films—*Platoon* and *Born on the Fourth of July*—to be fake, posturing rather than authentically anti-war. Oliver is a far more interesting and talented man than the mediocre John Kerry, but the filmmaker and the senator share this essential fraudulence. Both of these privileged Yalies volunteered to fight in Vietnam when virtually everyone on the campus already thought the war was wrong and was busy protesting it. My suspicion, though I cannot prove it, is that they enlisted in bad faith. Stone and Kerry knew that there was more to be gained on a personal level—for their professional advancement—by a predetermined strategy of going to fight and then returning to tell everyone how bad it was.

For me, Stone has always been the classic "Hollywood radical"—his espoused progressive political ideals in near complete opposition to his private behavior. His arrests for drug possession and driving under the influence are well documented, but they are the least of it. They are personal excesses engaged in by many, although perhaps not always to Oliver's extent. Nor is his drug use in the slightest hypocritical. He was, as many of us were, an avowed experimenter. You can judge that as you will. I take a rather libertarian view of drugs, especially where adults are concerned, and am not convinced that the "war on drugs" is of any use. What I am referring to here is not a psychedelic lifestyle or, for that matter, testing the limits of outré sex with consenting adults. I am talking about how he treated those closest to him—friends, family, and colleagues. Some part of me resisted telling the story that follows, but the play-acting of Hollywood liberalism reveals itself most clearly in this extraordinary divide between the public persona and the private person.

The phone rang one night around ten while Renee and I were lying in bed reading and watching TV. It was Oliver's wife Elizabeth—a nice, rather naïve Tippy Hedren lookalike—calling from their house. Renee was apparently one of her few friends and she would call once in a while to seek counsel on how to deal with the unpredictable Oliver. Tonight was more than the usual, though. With my ear half-cocked to the one side of the conversation I could hear, I gathered that Elizabeth was hysterical. In fact, I could hear her sobbing. She had discovered Oliver's diary.

This must have been 1986, because Oliver was in the midst of making *Wall Street*, released the following year. Renee signaled to me that what she was hearing was incredible. When she hung up, she filled me in. Elizabeth had read her portions of the diary. Oliver repeatedly described leaving the *Wall Street* set at lunch break for a Chinatown whorehouse where he had unprotected sex with several prostitutes. This was at the height of the AIDS epidemic. He was clearly putting his own wife at tremendous risk. He also had a two-year old son with Elizabeth. No wonder she was beside herself. It was hard for me to have much respect for the man again. That disconnect between the execrable private person and the self-important director who sought to define political morality for us with film portraits of Kennedy, Nixon, Castro, and, more recently, Mahmoud Ahmadinejad and George W. Bush, is unbridgeable for me. I could only laugh when I read that his key to the understanding of Bush was reformed alcoholism.

Stone's fascination with leaders, totalitarian and otherwise, is no doubt an outgrowth of his own narcissistic personality, but that makes him far from unique in Hollywood. I've seen many attracted to Castro in particular, even though these same people would have been incarcerated (or worse) had they lived in the Comandante's Cuba. Over the years, many of those same movie people have gone on clandestine, though in reality not all that risky, excursions to that benighted and forbidden country. A close director friend of mine told me that his wife veritably swooned when she met Fidel, kissing him on the cheek. The friend told me the story in amusement. I thought it was funny, too. Normally his wife was anything but totalitarian and would never have dreamed of planting a kiss on the cheek of, say, Heinrich Himmler. But something about Fidel got a pass—a certain Hollywood-style glamour mixed with nostalgia for a radical idealism that could only exist in the imagination.

I was in no way immune to this myself. My own fascination with Cuba dated back to 1960 when, at age sixteen, I went to see the victorious Castro speak in Central Park. That was the visit during which he famously roasted a chicken in his room in Harlem's Hotel Theresa. I remember vividly jostling with the largely Latino crowds that night, many of them Dominicans, yelling, "Viva! Viva!," urging Fidel to free their country the way he had Cuba. Castro harangued them passionately (and at length, of course) from a platform erected on Sheep Meadow, not more than fifty yards from the jungle gym where I'd played as a child. It was a stirring and politically powerful experience, before any of us had second thoughts about Castro or knew what he would do. Tears in my young eyes, I considered him a liberator from a fascist dictator. In college, I read about the Venceremos Brigades and thought about signing up to go and support the revolution, but I knew that my participation would be pointless and possibly personally embarrassing. Scarsdale boys weren't particularly good at cutting cane.

I finally visited Cuba myself in early 1979 in a less physically taxing capacity as a delegate to the First Festival of the New Latin American Cinema. I didn't get to meet the Comandante, but I did have an encounter with left-wing celebrities Regis Debray—Che Guevara's renowned French intellectual confidante and hagiographer—and Gabriel García Márquez—the Nobel Prize novelist and intimate of Castro. Through them I got to feel personally the magical pull of this kind of radical hero worship.

In fact, my entire trip to Cuba was of a romantic, or perhaps pseudo-romantic, sort, sneaking into the country semi-legally (it was never clear) on a chartered six-seater out of Miami. Ring Lardner Jr. of the Hollywood Ten was also aboard. Fortunately, the pilot—a Vietnam vet who was virulently anti-communist—didn't have a clue who the writer was, because he'd almost turned around when we approached Havana Airport. The presence of the old-time communist might have sealed the deal. The pilot was frustrated that the air traffic controllers didn't speak English—they didn't have a lot of U.S. flights in those days—and was treating the controllers' linguistic deficit as some kind of trick. I had to talk him into continuing, assuring him I spoke Spanish and could translate. It was a risky claim, because Cuban Spanish is rapid fire and I could barely understand the controllers. Still, we made it in.

That very night I met Debray and Márquez, when I was riding up alone in the elevator of the Hotel Nacional. It stopped at the mezzanine and two men I didn't immediately recognize—although one seemed vaguely familiar—got on. Trying to practice my Spanish, I made some small talk, explaining that I was there for the film festival. They told me they were, too, and were on the jury. It was then that I asked their names. Politics aside, just meeting the author of One Hundred Years of Solitude—one of the masterpieces of the twentieth century—was a powerful experience. I nearly gasped when he introduced himself, suppressing—and this is the key point—what knowledge I might have had of his relationship with Castro, the villa and chauffeured Mercedes that he'd supposedly been granted by the Maximum Leader while other authors—often liberal or leftist Cubans themselves—were exiled, jailed, or murdered. My director friend's wife didn't think about these things, either, when she kissed the dictator on the cheek.

Even with Debray, I stood there, more or less in awe, although I knew in general terms in 1979 that the man was Che's most famous apologist and that Guevara had been responsible for the ruthless killings of many of his one-time allies (*Al Paredon!* Up against the wall!), that he had helped create forced labor camps (though I didn't know, at that point, that they were used to "rehabilitate" homosexuals), the whole totalitarian bag of tricks borrowed from Stalin and Mao and conveniently overlooked in legend and popular culture like the recent puerile leftist fantasy *The Motorcycle Diaries*.

Yet I still shook the hand of Che's father, who was there for the occasion. After all, how could I resist? He was a celebrity. The other film festival delegates—including *Harlan County USA* director Barbara Koppel—obviously felt the same way, lining up to pump the hand of the great revolutionary's father not far from the square where a massive mural of Che himself dominated the already decaying city of Havana. (Interestingly, when I was there, one could not hear the fabulous Cuban music later made famous by *The Buena Vista Social Club* and other recordings. It was forbidden. Moses Wine's desire to hear it formed the basis of the only Wine short story I ever wrote, "Just Say No." In it, Moses is busted for smoking marijuana in front of the Hotel Nacional and is able to talk his way out of incarceration by sharing his love of Tito Puente with a member of the People's Police.)

Cuba itself, it was clear then, was a kind of giant jail of once-ornate homes and run-down DeSotos, its people sad, desperate, and undernourished. Anyone could see that. The question was how one reacted to the hopelessness. Was it simply that America was to blame? Evil Uncle Sam choking a nice Caribbean socialism with a vicious economic boycott? For some liberals and leftists that may have been the case, but I suspect that many of Fidel's apologists knew it wasn't that simple. But their minds were hijacked by their own mixed feelings—a cocktail of guilt, self-image, and rebellion that made it difficult to condemn Communist Cuba. My own view now is that although Cuba was undoubtedly an island-sized jail, the economic embargo was a tactical mistake. The power of the market would have overthrown Castro faster than all the

CIA agents in Langley squared. And it would have been better for the Cuban people as well.

For many years I was in the grip of the romantic fascination of that trip—the "privilege" of being "behind the Iron Curtain." It was my first such journey, with others to China (quite soon) and the Soviet Union still to come. I remember standing on the pristine Playa Jibacoa with members of our group, Cuban and American filmmakers, singing "Mira Que Linda Es Cuba" (Look How Beautiful Is Cuba) with tears in my eyes. And it *was* beautiful, a gorgeous beach and island unspoiled by the development that wrecks most of the world and that already, no doubt, is jeopardizing Cuba. The moment the embargo is over—Hello, Miami! At least communism did something in its economic backwardness, shielding one glorious Caribbean island from the worst aspects of modernity for a few decades.

My nostalgia for communism Cuban-style didn't really disappear, although it had abated, until I started to work with the actor Andy Garcia late in the 1990s. Andy was born in Havana and his grandfather had been an official of the Batista regime. The actor readily acknowledged the evils of Batista, but he'd also experienced Castro's own brand of totalitarianism on family and societal levels and had been developing a film for several years to express his feelings about the Cuban Revolution. That film—*The Lost City*, written by exiled Cuban novelist Cabrera Infante—was unfinanced at that point.

Andy and I were working on a script I had written, *The Gardener*, which I was to direct. *The Gardener* was a contemporary Los Angeles version of the classic *The Bicycle Thief*, with the protagonist an illegal alien gardener from Central America. Although very much an art film by Hollywood standards, it was pretty conventional liberal fare in its siding with the underclass and I was surprised that Andy, who was known in the Industry for his (rare) conservative political views, wanted to do it. We never got the money to make *The Gardener*, but I learned a lot about Cuba from Andy. He was and is a great ambassador of the culture and a producer of Cuban music, principally for the legendary bass player Cachao.

It was disappointing to me that *The Lost City*, when it was finally filmed, wasn't the movie that I know Andy wanted to make. The true story of the Cuban Revolution, sentimentalized in Sydney Pollack's phony *Havana* and briefly touched on in *Godfather II*, is a tale waiting to be told. Part of that tale, however, is the pivotal role of hero worship in the prosecution of revolutions, in the Cuban case of both that man of many t-shirts Che Guevara and the bearded, cigar-smoking Fidel Castro. This hero worship has a component of sexualized charisma that seems to be able to transcend ideology and even basic good sense. For all his family history, not even Andy Garcia was immune to it. Occupying a place of honor amidst the memorabilia on Andy's office wall is an original photo of those two bearded, cigar-smoking amigos—Ernest Hemingway and Fidel Castro.

I ran into an earlier—and almost blackly comic—version of this strange idolatry in the mid-Seventies in the persona of Huey P. Newton, co-founder (with Bobby Seale) and leader of the Black Panther Party. Though I did meet other Panthers, I never met Huey, but I was there as two Hollywood screenwriters plotted and helped execute his escape to Cuba. In those days (1974), Dyanne and I were friends with the writer-director Paul Williams (*The Revolutionary*) for whom I'd written a screenplay at Warner Brothers. Paul was then living in a small house on the outskirts of Malibu where he was working on a script with Artie Ross, a young man from a wealthy New York family. Ross was also part of the crowd of Bert Schneider, the son of one-time Columbia Pictures president Abraham Schneider, who had produced *Easy Rider* and the anti-Vietnam War documentary *Hearts and Minds*.

The subject of Paul and Artie's script was the escape from the U.S. of an Abbie Hoffman-like wanted radical. Whenever we came out to Malibu, they asked Dyanne and me to read the pages they had written for feedback. I remember those pages seeming particularly awkward and unreal, almost Hollywood phony. ("Do they really have rapids on the Rio Grande?" I recall asking. "Don't people just *walk* over the border there?") Ironically, at the same time Paul and Artie were working on this script, the two men, especially Artie, were involved in getting the *real* Huey Newton out of the country to Cuba. Their tales of how this escape was actually happening were fascinating—and, of course, should have been the movie, not their concocted fictional version. (I told them that, but they demurred, claiming they didn't want to put the real venture at risk.)

Apparently Artie had been given or somehow loaned—this was never clear—a sailboat by his rich father. This boat had been transported secretly to the Port of New Orleans for Newton to sail to Havana. Not far out, however, the inexperienced Huey had gotten the boat stuck on a sandbar. Soon enough, the Coast Guard showed up, finding themselves face-to-face with Huey P. Newton, then one of the most wanted men in America and internationally famous from the dramatic photo of him seated in an African wicker chair sporting a black beret while clutching a rifle in one hand and a spear in the other. The Coast Guard didn't recognize him. Huey told them he was out fishing and had gotten stuck. Friendly guys, the Coast Guarders offered to tow his boat off the sandbar, which they did.

Artie and Paul enjoyed recounting for Dyanne and me how the dumb Coast Guard had helped Huey Newton escape to Cuba. Omitted from their discussion was what Huey might be escaping from. It wasn't exactly revolutionary. Huey had been charged with murdering a seventeen-year-old prostitute. He came back from Cuba in 1977—some say because he didn't like it there; he says because the climate in the U.S. had changed—to face that charge, which ended in a mistrial. Several other accusations against Newton ended similarly. No doubt some of these prosecutions were overzealous. No doubt the government occasionally crossed the line into provocation when infiltrating the Panthers. No doubt Huey and the others did some good things like starting the children's breakfast program in Oakland and Watts. But Newton was no saint. Far from it. He dealt drugs, loved and lived violence, and eventually died in a battle over a cocaine deal in an Oakland housing project in 1989.

Artie Ross, however, expired before Huey even made it back from Cuba in 1977. The New York rich boy wannabe screenwriter—who I remember as mild-mannered and slightly nervous—was a great lover of laughing gas and kept a canister of nitrous oxide at the ready at his house. You weren't supposed to strap the nitrous mask to your face, but Artie, for whatever reasons, did anyway. One day, he never got it off. The joke in Hollywood was that he died laughing.

6 PAUL AND THE DAYS OF SUCCESS

I often told friends of mine that the man I most envied in the movie business was Paul Mazursky. This was in the early Eighties, around the time he made *Tempest* and *Moscow on the Hudson*, and what I envied about Paul was his remarkable ability to make personal films in Hollywood, personal films about subjects that interested me. He was able to have the career of a European auteurist director in the U.S. For that reason he was known as the West Coast Woody Allen.

I knew Paul slightly at that time. We would go to annual Fourth of July family picnics at a park in Brentwood where our kids played together. I would join in a pick-up basketball game with Paul and I could see right then he didn't like to lose, probably one of the secrets to his success. Every year or so, too, I sent Paul my latest Moses Wine crime novel in manuscript, hoping that he would turn it into a movie. Of all the directors I could think of, he seemed to have the closest sensibility to my novels—the Jewish humor, the liberal politics. He read them, sometimes even flirted with the idea of making them, but always ended up sending a complimentary Dear John letter. I kept trying, however.

Those were the years too that the books were getting a fair amount of attention. I had broken a long hiatus after *Peking Duck* with *California Roll* in 1986, in which private eye Moses Wine sells out and takes a corporate job as the security director of Tulip Computer, a thinly disguised Apple. (The novel begins with a variant on the old joke, "I never sold out before because nobody ever asked me.") The book was probably the first detective novel set in the burgeoning high-tech world of the Silicon Valley and echoed my own early fascination with computers. I ascribe this interest to the day in 1980 that Michael Schultz, the director of *Bustin' Loose*, walked into our production office in Universal Studios lugging a Lanier Computer the size of a steamer trunk. When I asked him what it was for, he told me it was to write down the screenplay. Screenwriter alarms of self-protection went off in my head. I had better learn how to use this behemoth or there was no telling what would happen to my script. (There was no telling anyway, but that was another matter.)

So it was out of self-defense that I became one of the first screenwriters to master the new technology of word processing, slogging my way through Wordstar, that primitive system which now seems like ancient calligraphy, trying to make it adapt to the screenplay format. In the midst of this, I fell in love with computers and soon enough was running through a variety of the early machines, including an Apple II, the clumsy "portable" Osborne with its minute screen and the magnificent Kay-Pro that resembled the oscilloscopes in my father's radiology office. I hooked these computers up to something new called a modem and used them as a crude terminal from which to communicate with other wannabe geek friends in arty Hollywood, such as Dr. Timothy Leary. I also was going on early online services like AOL and CompuServe, where I was the host of one of the first mass online author interviews. The subject was *California Roll*, and several hundred people joined in. In retrospect, it isn't as surprising as it sometimes seems to me that I was a relatively early blogger and chief executive of one of the first online news and blog aggregations, Pajamas Media. I am my father's son—an early adopter.

After *California Roll* came *The Straight Man*, a novel drawn from my experiences working with comedian Richard Pryor and from (too many?) years of psychotherapy. In *The Straight Man*, Moses Wine gets his case from his shrink—another detective novel first, I believe. I sent that manuscript to Mazursky as well. I assumed he'd be interested in this one because his films are filled with therapists. (In *Down and Out in Beverly Hills*, even the dog has a shrink.) But he passed on *The Straight Man*, too, although the Mystery Writers of America nominated the book for the Best Novel Edgar of 1987. My competition was the two British "Queens of Crime," P. D. James and Ruth Rendell. (Rendell won.) After that came *Raising the Dead*, the novel about Israel that I'd intended to write years before. But before I could send that one to Mazursky, I received a phone call from him that would change my movie career.

Paul called to ask if I had read the Isaac Bashevis Singer novel *Enemies,*

A Love Story. As it happened, I *had* read it—and quite recently—but he asked me to read it again, to "see if it might be a movie." Paul did this in a polite, almost formal manner—we still didn't know each other that well then—although his words had more impact than they might suggest. He knew and I knew that he was a power in the Industry, and a power of an unusual kind in that he loved and wanted to create film art of the highest order. Paul revered Fellini, Renoir, and the best of European art cinema and wanted to replicate what they did in the U.S. He was one of the few people on the planet, possibly one of only two (with Woody Allen) in the American film industry, who had the skills *and* the reputation to make a movie of the Singer novel, cited when the author won the Nobel Prize for Literature in 1978. I was reasonably certain that Mazursky was offering the opportunity of a lifetime to adapt this book. Well, not quite of a lifetime, because Warren Beatty had dangled the opportunity to write *Reds*—but something told me this was more serious.

I was correct. I quickly reread *Enemies* and turned up in Mazursky's office a couple of days later. Despite secretly feeling intimidated by the wall filled with Academy Awards and other diplomas for films like *An Unmarried Woman*, *Bob and Carol and Ted and Alice*, and *Harry and Tonto*, I stayed levelheaded enough and got the job collaborating with Paul on the screenplay of *Enemies*.

As I was to find out, that meant a "Hollywood-style collaboration," wherein the writer goes home and does most of the work while the director shares the credit, perhaps doing a polish at the end. That was the way Paul and I collaborated for the most part on all the films we wrote together—produced and unproduced. We'd sit down and block out the story, then I'd go home and actually write it down. At the end, the screenplay has a dual credit with an ampersand, indicating that the writers worked as a team.

I'm not angry with Paul about this. Hollywood runs on its own internal power game and pecking order. If you want to work with someone important, you play by those rules. I was comfortable collaborating in this manner with Paul because the material we worked on was vastly more interesting than the majority of movie business swill, and he was a superb director with "bankability." He was also an amusing companion, and soon a good friend. He allowed my name to appear before his on the script's title page, a tacit acknowledgement of authorship. And it paid well.

My compromise was made easier by the fact that most intelligent people in the Industry knew this was how the game was played. Many of them played it themselves. They knew how the credit, and the blame, should be dispensed. (It's interesting to speculate on the role of Hollywood liberalism when considering the "bad faith" of this sort of compromise. But it should be noted power games of this kind are played by movie people on both ends of the political spectrum.) On only one occasion do I recall really feeling strange about this arrangement—the night of the 1989 Academy Awards. But I get ahead of myself.

My task was to adapt *Enemies, A Love Story*. I broke down the novel for myself. It's an astonishing black comedy that reduces the Holocaust to the most human level. In 1949 New York, Herman Broder, a "ghost writer for a Rabbi," is married to his family's Polish servant woman, Yadwiga, who'd hid him from the Nazis during the war. Bored by the peasant Yadwiga, he's having an affair with the beautiful, brilliant, and neurotic Masha, a refugee from Auschwitz, who wants to marry him. While he lives this dual life, his own wife, Tamara, whom he believed killed by the Nazis, appears in New York, making Herman potentially a man with three wives.

As I told people later, it was "Feydeau meets the Holocaust," only it was derived from actual incidents that Singer had witnessed in New York after the war. People's husbands and wives did come from back from the dead, interrupting normal unruly existence.

Clever as this conception was, the novel's narrative did not translate easily into film. It had a picaresque quality, perhaps due to its having been written in serial form, almost ad hoc, for the *Forward* newspaper. I was troubled by how to solve this until I noticed that the story really caught fire about eighty percent of the way in, when Tamara, the dead wife, appears in New York. So I did something relatively brave—I restructured the work of a Nobel Prize winner, moving events that occurred close to page two hundred in the novel up to page twenty in the screenplay. Conventional wisdom—I think accurate in this instance—has it that some inciting incident has to occur about twenty minutes into a movie (screenplays usually time out at about a page a minute) that makes the protagonist's life irreversible. His wife returning from the dead seemed to fill that bill. It also solved the screenplay for me and I wrote it with surprising rapidity.

The movie—filmed eighteen months later after having been rejected at over twenty movie studios and financial entities—was almost verbatim what I wrote in just over three weeks. *Premiere Magazine* declared it statistically the best-reviewed movie of 1989. It was nominated for three Academy Awards, won the New York Film Critics best director prize, and has appeared on lists of the One Hundred Greatest Films of all time in the *New York Times* and the *Los Angeles Times*. But I cannot claim all the glory here, even faintly. Singer's novel is filled with brilliant interchanges between the characters, which I lifted intact. Also, Mazursky did an excellent, probably his best, job of directing a first-rate cast, featuring Ron Silver, Angelica Huston, and Lena Olin.

Along the way, however, were many frustrating and amusing incidents. Disney "developed," in Industry parlance, the screenplay and was therefore the first to read it. The script was declared well written in studio "coverage," but Disney head Michael Eisner asked Paul if the director couldn't update it, the way he had *Down and Out in Beverly Hills* (updated from the French classic *Boudu Saved from Drowning*). When Paul, nonplussed, replied that the Holocaust had only occurred in the Forties, Eisner, leery of historical films, recommended another more contemporary event. "What about the Afghani Holocaust?" said the Disney CEO.

Unfortunately, he wasn't joking. Not long after that, the script went into that special Hollywood purgatory known as "turn around" (rejected and returned to the producer). Paul soldiered on, going to many financiers. Several, in tried and true Hollywood fashion, wanted us to add a happy ending. (Hitler reroutes the cattle cars from Auschwitz to San Tropez. April Fools!) After months of this exercise in head banging, Joe Roth, then running Morgan Creek Productions at Twentieth Century Fox, greenlit the movie. No changes were ever made.

In February 1989, I got a phone call from my ex-wife Dyanne at 5:30 in the morning informing me that I'd been nominated for an Oscar. Somehow, she'd found out ahead of me. From then until the Award ceremony about a month later I was in a daze. The Academy Awards are an overwhelming event and something of an out-of-body experience. I don't remember very well what happened, even though I never expected to win. *Driving Miss Daisy*—a competent but pedestrian exercise in feel-good liberal pabulum of precisely the kind the Academy likes—was nominated in my category. In dramatic form, it had already won its author a Tony Award. Still, you live in hope.

Not that I admitted that to any of my friends. I told them Alfred Uhry (the *Daisy* playwright) was a sure winner—it had a Best Picture nomination, which we didn't—and that I was "surprised and honored to be nominated." I think for writers—excepting the likes of Gore Vidal or Norman Mailer—the experience of the Academy Awards is too much attention and glamour for our solitary existences. We aren't used to being in front of a billion people on television. By Oscar night, I was on a form of willed autopilot, mixed with strange bursts of megalomania that popped up like random spikes in an electro-cardiogram. In the limousine over with Mazursky, his wife Betsy and my then girlfriend Pamela Fong, I remember fantasizing that I *could* win, that Academy members were smart and would choose the complex *Enemies* over the more conventional *Daisy*. At that point, I went into silent anger toward Paul for stealing my sole credit. I wanted my Oscar alone. No matter that Paul had been unfairly deprived of a Best Director nomination (when he'd already won the prize from the New York Film Critics for the movie). I was in the land of ego.

But the rage was short-lived. By the time we reached the Los Angeles Music Center, I was overcome by a burst of klieg lights, walking along the storied red carpet past the likes of Tom Cruise, Daniel Day-Lewis, Michelle Pfeiffer, Denzel Washington, Kenneth Branagh, and Oliver Stone—all of whom were being buttonholed for television interviews. As I expected, they had no interest in me. (Japanese TV had interviewed Paul and me the day before, but U.S. networks had a more "balanced view" of the importance of writers.) I was relieved. I don't think I'd have been able to speak coherently, anyway. The rest was the blur referred to above. I remember sitting in the same row as Jessica Lange and Robin Williams. But that was only temporary; as I learned, we were all moved around during commercial breaks. The Academy Awards were a form of musical chairs, with the celebrity audience constantly shuttled about to accommodate presenters and awardees. I was in so much of a daze I don't even remember who presented the Best Adapted Screenplay when *Miss Daisy* won.

As you can see, I have ambivalent feelings about the Academy Awards themselves, but there is no question a nomination is hot currency in Hollywood. I could be cynical and say—for ten minutes. In truth, its afterglow can last a few years. It did for me, even though Paul and my next film, *Scenes from a Mall*, was a failure. Not that it should have been. At first the stars seemed in alignment for an immense success—a rare combination of commercial and artistic triumph.

The basics of the story were hammered out at the Farmers Market. Paul and I had daily breakfast with a group of writers, directors, and journalists—some "civilians" as well—at this Los Angeles landmark at the intersection of Fairfax Avenue and Third Street. It was actually considered Paul's table, since he was the most famous of us, but soon visiting grandees would stop by, including the most revered European directors when they came to town, and the table started generating a reputation as the Algonquin West. The BBC put it in a documentary about Hollywood, and my oldest friend, the playwright and screenwriter David Freeman, used the doings at the table in his book *It's All True: A Novel of Hollywood*. It also appears as the opening location in my *Director's Cut*, where I fantasize that Moses Wine is among the Hollywood hangers-on who gather at the table immediately after 9/11. Paul and I used it explicitly for our unproduced screenplay *Freddie Faust*, about a screenwriter who makes an unfortunate deal with a Bill Gates-like Mephistopheles to get his waning career back.

Like most things, the table at the Farmers Market is not what it once was, as people have grown older and drifted away. With a new family and obligations at Pajamas Media, I no longer go. In any case, my current political views are not particularly welcome at what remains of the table—where a sarcastic version of the most traditional liberalism reigns. I miss the camaraderie, however, and stay up on events there with David Freeman on our Saturday morning hikes in the Hollywood Hills.

The conception of *Scenes from a Mall* began at the Market and continued on private walks that Paul and I would take. We were trying to figure out the mystery of long marriages, how they ebbed and flowed and dealt with the eternal issue of fidelity. I had had a long one—by Hollywood standards, anyway—for fifteen years to Dyanne, and Paul's marriage to Betsy had been one of the longest I knew. Mine had ended in divorce, with fidelity as an issue; his endured. The subject matter was serious, with its echoes of Strindberg and Ingmar Bergman (the eventual title was an obvious homage to his *Scenes from a Marriage*), but knowing Paul and me some of the treatment would be comic. We had many concepts for how to structure this, but it was Paul's idea to reduce the primary speaking roles to just the couple and to put them in a mall, that most middle class and middle American of environments.

My early drafts of the screenplay were far more serious than the finished movie. At times they veered off in the darkly absurdist direction of Beckett or Pinter, with Deborah and Nick, the married couple, interacting with the glum stichomythia of Vladimir and Estragon of *Waiting for Godot*. I did this quite deliberately, feeling confident and willing to take risks with conventional cinematic style after *Enemies*, but Paul thought these exchanges too artsy and edited them from the script. We will never know who was right, because the film was eviscerated in production.

The story of the wreck of *Scenes from a Mall* is amusing (to others) and easy to understand on Hollywood terms. Everyone was interested in working with Paul and me after *Enemies*. Because of his relationship with Disney—*Down and Out in Beverly Hills* was their most successful production of that era—we went to them first. Jeffrey Katzenberg was then running the studio for Michael Eisner. This was before the two had a very public falling out and Katzenberg went on to form Dreamworks with David Geffen and Steven Spielberg. Jeffrey said yes to developing *Scenes from a Mall* immediately. I can't believe the meeting in and out took more than fifteen minutes, and that included the usual small talk, offers of Perrier, and so forth. The truth is that a successful Hollywood pitch meeting rarely takes longer than that. Usually it has more to do with who you are than what you're selling. If they want to work with you, chances are they will make the deal. If they don't, you can have the best idea of all time and they probably won't. In this case they wanted to work with us *and* we had a good idea. It was a slam-dunk.

While we were working on *Scenes*, Paul and I speculated on who would play Nick and Deborah. The roles called for dramatic mood swings as each in turn revealed his or her infidelity and therefore required the ability to switch from high melodrama to near farce in seconds. One obvious choice was Jack Nicholson and Anjelica Huston, a couple with a checkered past of their own, and both of whom were magnificent actors. But more and more we saw Meryl Streep in the role of Deborah. It was difficult to decide who would play opposite her—we kept changing our minds—but Streep, we agreed, was ideal for the female lead. Sam Cohn, the legendary agent at ICM in New York, represented Paul and Meryl. Sam had been a strong advocate for *Enemies* during the struggle to get it produced. (The agent apparently told his therapist he identified with the protagonist—a man married to three women.) Paul decided to give the script to Sam who would "slip it" to Streep before the studio had even read it. He did, and we were told that she liked it and would do the movie.

Paul and I were ecstatic. We delivered the script to the studio. They liked it, too. We even heard that Michael Eisner proposed that Paul direct it on Broadway first as a two-character production. I was intrigued, but Paul declined. (The script was produced as a play in Holland many years later.) We went in for a production meeting with Katzenberg. Jeffrey in those days may have been the hardest working executive in Hollywood. He was famous for double booking breakfasts or calling people at six in the morning to find out what projects they were working on, what scripts might soon be available. Not for nothing was he called the "Golden Retriever." He was the kind of person you loathed for his naked ambition but respected for his energy. Most of all he had confidence in his own power. In that meeting he immediately asked who would play the couple. Paul said that Streep was interested and Jeffrey nodded. It was hard to tell whether he liked this idea or not. Then he inquired about the male lead. We gave him a list of names, including Nicholson, Kevin Kline, and, I think, Harrison Ford. Katzenberg then asked: What about Woody?

Woody Allen? Paul and I were nonplussed. Woody didn't do other people's movies—at least not since *The Front*, which had been about thirteen years before, before Woody was, well, Woody. At that point, 1989, he was regarded as close to the most important active filmmaker in world cinema, the *auteur* of *auteurs*, having already written, directed, and starred in *Sleeper, Love and Death, Annie Hall, Manhattan, Zelig* (my favorite), *Broadway Danny Rose*, and *Hannah and Her Sisters*, to name only a few. Nevertheless, Katzenberg said he had been speaking with Woody and, given this script with Paul directing, he might do it. We should go home and think it over.

I would like to say we thought it over, but of course we didn't—at least I didn't, and I strongly suspect Paul didn't much, either. This was

Woody Allen, after all, the "King of the Jews." (We'd call him that on the set, although not to his face, of course.) Paul and I said a few words to each other about Allen not really being an actor, about Woody always being Woody no matter who he played. Perhaps, we thought, our character required an actual trained performer who could act roles. The script called upon Nick to break down in tears, among other extreme emotional moments. But this talk was perfunctory and we both knew it. We wanted Woody with a fever. Paul allowed a brief period to go by—probably no more than a day—and gave Katzenberg the go ahead to approach Allen.

Normally a movie star takes at least a week or two, often a lot longer, to respond to an offer of work. The star doesn't want to appear overly available, even to a major studio from which the offers are of large numbers that only they can afford. Woody answered in a weekend. He would do it. I think I grew a foot when I heard it, feeling about as close to invulnerable as I ever had in my life. Say what you will about hubris—it's fun for a minute. Then we got a message from Sam Cohn, who represented Woody as well and was in on the minutiae of the process: Meryl Streep had changed her mind. She wouldn't do the movie with Woody. Paul and I had avoided the obvious fact that Meryl, having worked with Allen on *Manhattan*, knew that Woody couldn't act. To his credit, Allen said as much to Paul in response to the script. He wasn't a real actor. He couldn't cry. He could just be himself.

At that point, I couldn't care less. Woody Allen was doing my script—and he wasn't even asking for changes. (He actually never altered a line or even ad-libbed one, except once or twice by accident.) Disney couldn't care less, either. It was clear that they never wanted Meryl in the first place. They wanted someone more commercial, funnier, to go with Woody. They wanted the star of Paul's hit *Down and Out in Beverly Hills*. They wanted Bette Midler. And in no time at all, they had her. Bette and Woody as a Christmas release for 1990. They'd be paid five million dollars each to portray Deborah and Nick Fifer, quite a munificent sum for that time, even for Hollywood.

And then, as they say, the troubles began—although you couldn't see them on the surface. Most of the problems seemed like superficial irritations at the time. Woody, well known to hate Los Angeles, refused to come here for any length of time. A screenplay that was written about a Hollywood Hills couple going to shop at the Beverly Center on Los Angeles's LaCienega Boulevard, was filmed in Los Angeles for just three days, the maximum Woody would tolerate. The rest was shot in a mall in Stamford, Connecticut, and on a soundstage in Queens, where the Beverly Center interior was meticulously and eerily reconstructed at ridiculous expense. Woody also demanded to be ferried back and forth to California in the Disney jet with his then significant other Mia Farrow and a number of their adopted children.

Power-tripping stars—so often those most known for their liberalism—selfishly running up the budget didn't surprise me. I had been in Hollywood too long. But I was taken aback by one thing: Woody Allen was a cold fish. With the exception of production photographer Brian Hamill, whose presence on the film was another Woody requirement, Allen rarely, if ever, talked casually to anybody on the set. He never palled around with the crew or the other actors, as most stars do to some degree. He didn't talk to me and he barely talked to Paul Mazursky when I was around. Nor did he work very hard. He'd shoot a couple of takes, then quickly say something like "You got it?" to Paul and make a move to walk off. No matter what, he was gone to his trailer by four.

I could tell that Paul didn't know how to deal with this. A fine actor himself, normally he was an actor's director and took pleasure in rehearsing and working with his actors. He got the excellent performances in *Enemies* that way. But he seemed intimidated by Woody (we all were), and even if he hadn't been, I don't know how he would have broken through. Making matters worse, there was absolutely no chemistry between Allen and Midler. The premise of the script was that they did love each other but had strayed, each briefly, in the course of a twenty-five-year marriage. The audience is supposed to *want* the marriage to survive, but to do that it has to imagine it having been good. It was impossible to imagine Woody ever having been attracted to Bette, especially the Bette of 1990. Unflatteringly costumed, she looked like somebody's Jewish aunt from Great Neck—the very thing Woody had been fleeing his entire life. Bette is not to blame in this. She gave it her all. But she was up against a man whose libido was otherwise engaged.

Perhaps we should have known where it was engaged, because that might have explained a lot of things about Woody's curious lack of artistic concentration, as well as further clarified his lack of interest in Bette

Midler. Allen was starting, or on the brink of starting, his own romantic melodrama of quasi-marital (he and Mia Farrow were never officially married) deception that was considerably more bizarre than anything I'd written in the screenplay. A Korean girl named Soon-Yi Previn made her first (uncredited) appearance as a film extra in *Scenes from a Mall*. Then all of twenty, she was the adopted daughter of André Previn and Mia, who in 1992 was revealed, through nude photos, to have been having an affair with Allen. The liasion between a much older (fifty-seven) man and a young woman who'd become his relative was splashed across the world's tabloids. Farrow split with Allen, accusing him of child molestation (not with Soon-Yi, but with another child they had mutually adopted), and Allen married Soon-Yi in 1997, almost as if to resurrect his own extremely tarnished reputation.

Did the Soon-Yi and Woody relationship begin during *Scenes from a Mall*? I have no proof, but the timeline and Woody's quick departures for his trailer make it highly likely. *Something* began then. The general decline of Woody Allen's film career dates from the period as well.

But none of this stopped Disney from loving the film—at least at first. Shortly after seeing the director's cut with Mazursky, I got a personal call from Katzenberg. He and Eisner had seen the cut too a few days later and thought it was great, going so far as to say it was the best film produced by the studio during their administration. I had never heard him so effusive. Frankly, I had had mixed feelings upon seeing it, but ascribed some of that reaction to being "too close to the project." In any case, what did it matter? Katzenberg and Eisner liked it. The critics and the public probably would too. What did I know?

As it turned out, a lot. The first previews of the movie, held in Pasadena and Granada Hills to be out of sight of the Hollywood crowd and critics, were close to a disaster, with audience report card numbers at the low end of the scale. Focus groups, those bêtes noires of filmmakers, were created to give the fans a chance to tell us how to solve the problem, to say what was missing for them. I knew what was missing for me—the performances were boring. The Fifers seemed about as much in love as Bill and Hillary Clinton. Maybe the script wasn't so hot, but I would never know. This wasn't remotely what had been conceived. I sat in those audiences next to Michael Eisner, of all people, trying to figure out how to rescue the project. He was surprisingly cheerful for the head of a company about to take a thirty-million-dollar bath. Maybe theme park revenues were up. Whatever the explanation, I had no idea how to fix the film and neither did Paul, although he didn't admit it. He was better at keeping a stiff upper lip than I was, even after the opening was postponed from the coveted Christmas spot to a less competitive one in February.

Just before the movie opened, Paul and I did the smart thing. We left town. For Nepal. Yes, when *Scenes from a Mall* was making its anemic debut across the U.S., its authors, Paul Mazursky and Roger Simon, were with two other friends—Michael Green and Jeff Taylor—in Kathmandu about to embark on a Himalayan trek. The Gulf War was beginning in Kuwait and Iraq, and much to the consternation of Michael Green, I carried a shortwave radio with me into the mountains to track events in the Middle East. Green, an actor, was tall and bore an uncanny resemblance to George H. W. Bush. (He often played him in commercials.) He was also an unreconstructed hippie—did about as much LSD in his time as the Grateful Dead—and was appalled that I was breaking the Buddhist quietude of our journey with vulgar war news. But I listened anyway, trying to be discreet as I held the radio to my ear in the tent our sherpa porters erected for us each night, glued to that news while in the other tent my companions laughed, ate popcorn, and smoked hash.

I had discovered something interesting about myself. I was no longer the kid who marched in front of the UN shouting, "Ho Ho Ho Chi Minh … Vietcong is gonna win!" I was a patriot who wanted *America* to win, who wanted people across the world to be free, to have what we have. Michael Green thought I had gone off the deep end. This is not to denigrate Michael, who is a loveable sort and in many ways paradigmatic of the Hollywood worldview, but—perhaps it was because I tried some of that Nepalese hash myself—I felt myself drifting away from something. Just as I was becoming successful in Hollywood, I was beginning to feel estranged from it—like Robert A. Heinlein's Mars-raised earthling returning to Earth in *Stranger in a Strange Land*.

Only months before I had felt even more like an earthling returned from Mars to Hollywood when I encountered—more specifically was hired and fired in twenty-four hours—the woman perhaps known as the greatest of all Hollywood liberals, Barbra Streisand. Barbra was a great admirer of *Enemies*. She had made a musical version of an I. B.

Singer novel herself, *Yentl*. (Singer didn't like it and had asked Mazursky to promise there would be no singing in our adaptation of *Enemies*.) Out of nowhere, I received a phone call from Streisand's producer and confidante Cis Corman asking if I'd read Pat Conroy's *The Prince of Tides*. I immediately suspected the reason—Barbra was known to be making a film from the novel. She was probably looking to have the script rewritten. I admitted that I hadn't read the book and a copy was messengered to me within hours. I read it as quickly as I could and a meeting was set up with Barbra at her house in Holmby Hills, a swanker-than-swank subdivision of Beverly Hills.

She met me in a white room, dressed all in white. There was something pristine and otherworldly about it, as if dust were not allowed to settle. Beside her were two cardboard boxes. Inside one were about seven or eight drafts of the screenplay with hundreds of pages of transcriptions of interviews Streisand had done with psychiatrists. As well as direct, the actress was to play Dr. Susan Lowenstein, a psychiatrist, in the movie. Many later remarked that she did a good job of this, except that she had longer and more meticulously manicured nails than any known psychiatrist. I noticed this, too, as she gestured to the boxes.

Most of the interviews were with one particular psychiatrist whose name now eludes me but was also something of an Indian mystic and lived in the California desert, practicing yoga. Evidently he was Barbra's guru of the moment. I failed to see how this person would be helpful with the characterization of a New York Jewish psychoanalyst, but was too polite to ask. Also, I wanted the job, even though I knew that working with Streisand would be no walk in the park. The other box contained videocassettes of the entire Joseph Campbell *Power of Myth* series on PBS. She wondered if I had seen it. She seemed disappointed when I said I'd only seen one, but she presented me with the box as further background research for *The Prince of Tides*.

I went home with more reading and viewing material than I'd ever had from a story meeting, and dutifully sat down and started to go through the most recent draft of the screenplay. You had to start somewhere. It was by Becky Johnston and seemed to be a worthy adaptation of the book. I was interrupted by a phone call from my agent. Would I be willing to share writing credit with Barbra? I groaned at the thought. She probably wouldn't write a word. But it was the nature of the game, so I said yes. At the very least this would be one for my memoirs, if I ever wrote them: my collaboration with Barbra Streisand. I had no idea how short it would be.

That night around 10:30 my phone rang. I wasn't used to getting calls at that hour, except for family and close friends, and was startled when the voice on the other end said, "Hello, this is Barbra." Barbara? *Barbara*? I didn't know any Barbaras. Oh my God, *that* Barbra, the one without the extra "a." The "People Who Need People" Barbra. The most powerful woman on cinema screen and concert stage, with whom I'd just met that afternoon. What was she doing calling at this hour? It crossed my mind that perhaps I had made a better impression than I realized—when she asked flatly if I'd read the screenplays yet. Specifically, she wanted to know what I thought of the second scene in the third draft.

Second scene in the third draft? I had read a couple of 120-page drafts that day, but not that one. I'd also skimmed through a few hundred pages of Barbra's tedious dialogue with her guru. I was a fairly fast reader, but not even Evelyn Wood herself could have come close to reading all the way through this material. When I told her that I hadn't had a chance to look at the third draft yet, there was a silence, after which she said, "Your agent is asking for too much money." Too much money? I hadn't even known the studio and my agent had opened negotiations, so had no idea what he was asking, if anything. When I gently told this to Barbra, there was another heavy silence. I had a feeling I was getting off on the wrong foot with Barbra Streisand.

I was correct. A third call came from my agent the next day informing me that Streisand was "moving on." I had been fired before being fully hired. Jack Rosenthal, her collaborator on *Yentl*, would be writing the script with her. (As it turned out, the script that was eventually shot was the Becky Johnston version.) Later in the day a case of Château d'Yquem showed up from Columbia Studios as a kind of consolation prize, I suppose. I enjoyed it, but I never bothered to watch the Campbell videos.

My biggest regret is that very soon thereafter I chucked the screenplay drafts and guru dialogues in the garbage. Those dialogues might be worth a lot on eBay today, as an example of hilariously puerile movie star blather. Streisand, like others of her ilk, was hugely talented artistically, but of marginal intellectual ability, entirely cliché-ridden in her thinking. This is worth remembering when reacting to her political pronouncements. I never had anything to do with Barbra after that encounter, but, thanks to the Drudge Report, I was made aware of her political website in recent years. One of her short postings in early 2006, mocking Bush as a C student and not surprisingly now removed from the Internet, had no fewer than eleven spelling errors. Among the misspelled words: "Iraq," "curruption," "warrented" and "subpoening." Some people are too grand perhaps even for spellchecker.

After the failure of *Scenes from a Mall*, Paul Mazursky and I worked on three other scripts that were commissioned by studios but never produced. Screenwriters often complain their best work was never filmed and they may be right. The first of the projects Paul and I worked on after *Scenes*—an adaptation of Bernard Malamud's *Pictures of Fidelman*—had a similar history of near misses. At least *Fidelman*—actually a collection of short stories about Arthur Fidelman, a Jewish American who goes to Italy in the Fifties to become a painter—took me to Rome twice, once for research and once to romance some financiers who were considering production.

We also worked on a script about the Dead Sea Scrolls and Jewish messianism, for which we visited Israel. I have fond memories of blithely driving our rental car through the West Bank, stopping in places like Ramallah and Jenin (this was 1993, when such things were possible) and talking with the locals. Paul seemed almost fearless, not acting as if he believed anything could happen. I was often more tense, perhaps from more knowledge of the area and the environment. I had spent time on the West Bank before while researching my novel *Raising the Dead*.

The third screenplay we developed was the aforementioned *Freddie Faust*, largely set at the Farmers Market. In many ways it was the most autobiographical, the kind of film Paul had done years before, like *Next Stop, Greenwich Village* or *An Unmarried Woman*, this time updating the classic Faust story of a man battling aging into our own familiar territory of screenwriters facing mortality.

I don't know for sure why none of these movies got made, but it is certain that Hollywood was changing all around us. These scripts had been developed for major studios and the industry was morphing into the era of the independents, when the studios rarely made serious films. We were in the Sundance era. I was a part of that myself, teaching screenwriting for several years in the early Nineties at Robert Redford's Sundance Institute in Sundance, Utah. These institutes lasted for about a week after which we teachers—professional screenwriters and directors—would return to our normal bailiwicks, usually New York or LA.

Sundance was a blissful environment, high in the Wasatch Mountains. One fine spring day a group of us rode on horseback with a guide up to the top of the ridge. "How much of this is Redford's?" I asked. "All of it," she said, gesturing across the tops of the mountains practically as far as the eye could see. The superstar of *Butch Cassidy* and *The Sting*, among other early hits, had obviously done well in his real estate dealings. I met Redford—known locally as "Ordinary" in ironic reference to his first directorial effort *Ordinary People*—the second day of my first year teaching there. I was in a small teacher's meeting, discussing our students—who were largely established published or producer writers from other media—when someone said something. I turned to see "Ordinary" sitting next to me in his signature jeans and work shirt—just one of the guys. He nodded to us and we went right on with the meeting.

I know I won't make friends by saying this, but I don't think Sundance has done all that much for film, either at the Institute or at the vaunted festival in Park City. Like Starbucks, it has institutionalized rebellion and originality into something weirdly conformist and conventional. Part of the reason for this is political, of course. There is an unexamined uniformity to the liberalism of the Sundance Film Festival that veers toward the comic. But it is more than that. Sundance feels more like a cult than it does like art. It didn't grow spontaneously as art does, but as if from a studied Petri dish with particular rules and values.

Redford complains about the commercialization of his festival. But that is the least of it. This problem is its preciousness. Sundance's relative failure can be seen in its paltry results. Not in its entire twenty-year history (since 1978) has it produced a single film with anywhere near the societal impact of *Chinatown*, *The Godfather*, *Star Wars*, *American Graffiti*, *Close Encounters*, or *E. T.*, to name just a few of the seminal movies of the Seventies, all of them produced in the belly of the major studio system. Nor has it been the instigator of the careers of any important *auteurs*— not that we have seen many in recent years, the one salient exception being Spain's Pedro Almodóvar.

Part of Sundance's difficulty is that it came along at a time when the art of film was in decline. The culture had moved on to blogs and computer games and myriad other diversions, real and imagined. That cannot be stopped or even slowed very much by a film festival. When I first saw that change taking place around me, I bemoaned it. Now I do not. Much as I love the cinema, it has its limitations. The dramatic film is, more than we admit, a superficial form and, in an odd way, dependent on its superficiality for its success. It is at its essence a quick emotional hit, a feeling that we are all engulfed with as we identify with the life on the screen, throwing ourselves into it. At its best (*Casablanca*, *The Seven Samurai*, *Nights of Cabiria*) this can be an inspiring experience with overtones of Aristotle's catharsis, but it is not necessarily deep or complex. Nor is it engaging to the audience, except in a passive way. The interactive computer arts of the future may reach the mind and the emotions on far more significant levels.

Now I admit some of this may be sour grapes. In 1997, I had my chance, directing a film about love and reconciliation after the Holocaust—*Prague Duet*—that my wife Sheryl and I wrote. It was meant to be serious art. Respectable though it was, it fell short. I could give a list of excuses for the relative failure—the wrong person cast, the German producer reneging on the money, etc., etc. But almost every film involves some kind of snafu. It comes with the territory of working in an art form that costs millions of dollars to produce.

Would I do it again? Yes, of course—though something would be missing. It doesn't mean quite as much. The world, as I said, has moved on. And so have I. One indication of this is that, as a member of the Motion Picture Academy, I receive DVDs of virtually all the year's English-language films in the hopes their producers and talent will win my Oscar vote. Starting in December, the discs roll in like the brooms in the "Sorcerer's Apprentice" scenes from *Fantasia*. When I was young, I would have jumped for joy. Imagine your father getting all the movies free for you to see. It would be like going to the 86th Street Grande, my childhood hangout, in my own house. Today, my ten-year old daughter mostly shrugs. Some of the movies are interesting to her, yes, but, a bright girl, for the most part she has other things to do. Reality television is often more appealing to her. She would rather see real people, modified and pumped up though they may be, in all their irregularities, than simplified fictional heroes.

I myself don't see many of the free movies. Come Oscar time, when I'm supposed to make my selection, I feel guilty. Sometimes I don't even vote. When I go to the Farmers Market now and look around at the old writers' table, it's as if I'm visiting what Proust would call "un autre moi." Paul Mazursky and I still talk. We're still friends and we love each other. But it is not the same.

7 THE INTERNATIONAL ASSOCIATION OF CRIME WRITERS, THREE TRIPS TO RUSSIA, AND HOW I CAME TO BE RECRUITED BY THE KGB

In 1987, when I was still living with my second wife, Renee, in Malibu, I received a letter from Mexico City, which had an immense effect on my life for several years, sending me around the world several times and even leading to my being solicited by the KGB—how seriously and with what intent I will never know.

The letter was handwritten in English by someone named Paco Taibo II, evidently a Mexican history professor and mystery writer. It alluded to him and his friends enjoying the movie of *The Big Fix* in Mexico City and invited me to come to Mexico to help form a group called the International Association of Crime Writers. They would pay for my ticket and there would be writers from both sides of the Iron Curtain. Among those invited, it said, were John le Carré, Georges Simenon, and Graham Greene.

I looked twice at the letter to see if I had read it correctly. Was this for real? Had I died and gone to mystery writer heaven? Perhaps it was a practical joke, but it was a strange one if it was. The postmark really *was* Mexican. The letter also mentioned a fourth writer—Julian Semyonov of the Soviet Union—whose name I didn't recognize. But that didn't matter. The first three names were sufficiently august for a Nobel Prize shortlist. I RSVPed that I'd come. In a few days, I had a letter back with a ticket enclosed. If it was a joke, it had just become several degrees more elaborate.

I was met at the Mexico City airport a couple of weeks later by a driver from the Ministry of Culture who chauffeured me on a winding five-hour trip to the state of Queretaro, the *altiplano* of Central Mexico. We continued through the colonial city of Queretaro—by now it was after ten at night; I had left Los Angeles later than I'd wanted because of movie commitments—to the nearby pueblo of San Juan del Rio, pulling up at a hacienda illuminated with spotlights. Paco Taibo II, a squat Sancho Panza-like man, came forward the moment I got out of the car (how did he know I was there?). Speaking in rapid-fire English while sucking on a cigarette and swilling Coke from the bottle—two things I'd learn the Mexican mystery writer was never without—he helped me deposit my bags in a suite (apparently I was staying with him) and led me upstairs to the second floor.

There, the Don Quixote atmosphere persisted as we headed down a corridor lined with portraits of ruff-collared nobles interspersed with shields and halberds to a banquet room where ten or so men and one woman were assembled around a long table. I was apparently the last to arrive. I scanned the group for some sign of le Carré, Simenon, or Greene, when a white, bearded hulk of a man in a safari jacket, a dead ringer for Hemingway or at least one of those Hemingway lookalikes from the plaza in Pamplona during the running of the bulls, came lumbering toward me.

"Simon, I am Semyonov!" he said, in a thick Russian accent, clasping me in one of the legendary bear hugs of his country. "We are brothers!"

I smiled noncommittally, unwilling to go quite that far just yet because of some similarity in our names, and waved my greetings to the group American-style. I was bidden to take a seat at the table and introduced to the other writers. Besides the man I would later find out was the best-selling author in the Soviet Union, there was a Pole, a Czech, a Rumanian, and three Cuban guys, one of whom—a short, beady-eyed Stalinist apparatchik type—appeared to be in charge of the other two, who kept looking at him nervously. This was supposed to be to be writers' group with people on both sides of the Iron Curtain, but it was clear it was tilted more than a little to the East, or East via the Caribbean.

Even the Western writers were decidedly leftist. I knew one of them by reputation, the Spanish intellectual Vázquez Montalbán, who had written the mystery *Murder in the Central Committee* and was one of the authors of the constitution of Eurocommunism. He was there with another Spaniard, Juan Madrid, actually *from* Madrid. I immediately suspected Juan was Jewish, because many Marrano families had taken city names. (It proved to be true.) Two of the others were Milanese publishers—Marco Tropea and the lone woman, Laura Grimaldi, elegantly dressed in the grand tradition of upper class Italian Marxists. Laura, it turned out, was known in her country's press as "Mother Courage" for her continual pilgrimages from Milan to the boot of Italy where her son was imprisoned as a member of the "Red Brigade."

Everyone was extremely welcoming as I sat down, acting as if we'd known each other for years in the great bonhomie of left-wing mystery writers. They enthusiastically filled me in on what I had missed of the meeting. This new organization was going to break ground, be the first writers' group with officers on both sides of that Curtain. We would show the way for the politicians—this was, as you will recall, 1987, the early days of *glasnost*—and I was being asked, said one of the Cubans, to be a member of the "Comité Central."

Say what? Co-mee-tay Sen-tral? It was very late, well past midnight, and, though still a bit nervous, I started laughing. If they wanted me to go back to the U.S. and organize American writers to join this nascent International Association of Crime Writers or *Associacion de Escitores Policiacos* (AIEP), as they called it, I explained to them in halting Spanish, this "central committee" dog would not hunt. The others at the table stared at me in confusion, except for Laura Grimaldi, who, from her expression, quite obviously understood.

"American writers won't join with that name," I went on. "It smacks of communist rhetoric. They'll worry about being blacklisted." Ah, *now* they got it. I had said the secret word—blacklist. Everybody knew about that. In truth, I was a bit worried about it myself.

At that point, Paco Taibo asked me what I suggested we call our group for the American audience. "The *Executive* Committee," I said. "That's what we call these groups back home. That would work." Ah, ah, all agreed—the *"comité executivo"* ... and so it was. I was to be North American Vice-President of this Executive Committee, or some such. Paco and Semyonov would be Co-Presidents. Montalban was named European Vice-President. Silly as this all was, I was flattered. I hadn't been an officer of anything then since seventh grade student council. And in a bizarre way it felt vaguely similar, play-acting like junior high school politics, even when Semyonov said that for our next meeting he would arrange for us all, plus some other "important writers" (pronounced "rye-terz") from the U.S. and Britain that I would help select, to come to the Soviet Union—their treat. Who "their" was I wasn't entirely sure, but it didn't matter. I didn't think it would ever happen. I suspected he was just showing off.

By now we were in the small hours of the morning, and, having come all the way from LA, I assumed it was time for bed. Not for this crowd. Not all of them, anyway. Juan Madrid announced that he was making a pilgrimage to an Indian whorehouse, evidently famous in the region for some reason, though I never caught the name of the tribe. We were invited to come along. Semyonov said that he'd go—it would be good research, a writers' duty. I could tell that the machismo of the one true gringo in the crowd was being challenged, so I went, too, a few of us wedging into a small car and driving over some mountain roads to a run-down roadhouse in the middle of nowhere.

The Indian cathouse felt like a throwback to another era with rickety wooden tables grouped around a dirt floor where local *braseros* danced a two-step to *ranchera* music with the Indian women, the latter dressed rather primly in plain smocks. When the dance stopped, the men went off with their partners to nearby rooms.

I sat at a table with Semyonov, trying to drink a foul pulque I could barely swallow that tasted something like rubbing alcohol. The Russian, not surprisingly, didn't have a problem with it. He wasn't interested in sex anymore, he explained with a laugh, patting his ample stomach, a holding tank for who knows how many gallons—or barrels—of vodka over the years, as if it made intercourse impossible (and who knows—it may have), but he could still drink. And could he ever. He continued to down one pulque after another as I sat there feeling nauseated and listening to bits of his life story.

Apparently, Julian had grown up near the seat of Soviet power, a fascinating but not always reassuring childhood. His father had been secretary to Nikolai Bukharin, the Politburo member executed by Stalin in 1937 when Semyonov himself was sixteen. His father was ostracized as an "enemy of the people," but that hadn't stopped young Julian. Semyonov managed to survive to write and publish a long and enduring series of first anti-Nazi and later anti-CIA thrillers starring Maksim Issaev, the Soviet James Bond. Adapted for several television series and movies, they made Julian a household name in the USSR and have enjoyed something of a revival, it should not be surprising, in Putin's Russia.

But I had only learned some of that that night when, on the way back to the hacienda, Julian leaned over to me and said confidentially in his thick accent, "Roger, I see you not believe I invite you to Russia this spring. You wonder how I bring many writers to my country for two weeks ... to see Red Square ... Yalta...." He paused for effect. "Some say I am colonel KGB, but...." But what, I might have asked. I didn't. I was feeling over my head. Besides, I didn't believe that anything of the sort was going to happen anyway. "But," Semyonov continued, "that is rumor. How could I be KGB and talk like this? I would be arrested!" He laughed and squeezed my shoulder. "You will be guest of Novosti Press Association."

Three months later, I sat in the lobby of Moscow's Cosmos Hotel, a grandiose but already down-at-the-heels post-Sputnik affair, complete with a blinking model satellite for a chandelier. With me were Paco Taibo and Laura Grimaldi. We were indeed guests (with about a dozen others from around the world) of the Novosti Press Association, an outfit supposedly on the "liberal" side of the *glasnost* struggle. Laura had been showing us what happened when she had gone to the ladies room, which was perhaps thirty meters across the expansive lobby. A heavy woman in black had appeared out of nowhere, tailing her across those entire thirty meters and into the lavatory. "She practically followed me into the stall," said Laura, more amused than shocked. "I had to bolt the door and tell her to go away. So she just stood just outside, smoking a cigarette." Now we were all staring at the woman in black who looked back at us blankly without the slightest hint of embarrassment. "She's a civil servant, poor thing," the Italian publisher continued. "It's an employment question. If these people weren't spies, they wouldn't have anything for them to do."

I'd been thinking the same thing. Ever since arriving at Moscow's Sheremetyevo Airport, I had been under the escort or surveillance of someone who seemed at least tangentially related to an intelligence agency. People would mysteriously appear and ask me questions, inquire how I was doing, and then disappear, never to be seen again. Meanwhile, we each had our own interpreter from Novosti. I had a curious gap-toothed little man named Oleg who'd been the translator for the Russian contingent at the Aswan Dam and seemed to be on first name basis with Gamal Abdel Nasser. Why was he interpreting for me? I could inflate my own ego as Hollywood Man, but I wondered. And Novosti itself—what was it, really? If they were so liberal, why did they need to follow us everywhere?

Well, not *everywhere*. Paco and I had taken off on the Moscow subway almost on arrival to check out the major sites of the city. In the interim, the three months between San Juan del Rio and Russia, the Mexican mystery writer and I had been forging a friendship, which would become quite deep. I'd even arranged to fly with Paco to Moscow. My ticket took me from LA to Mexico City where I met the Coke-guzzling Mexican writer and rode with him—on a shaky Aeroflot jet resembling a cattle car—via Havana to the Russian capital. Even so, I was suspicious of Paco. Who was he in all this? We seemed to be in a den of spies. Was Paco—a born organizer if ever I'd met one—one of them, an agent of Cuban intelligence, perhaps? (Years later, Paco wrote a Che hagiography called *Ernesto Guevara: Tambien Conocido Como El Che*.) A meeting had been held in Havana, I'd learned, before San Juan del Rio, in which Paco had participated, at which the idea of the International Association of Crime Writers had been formulated. This wasn't proof of anything, but it was more than a little bit suspicious. Perhaps I was being gulled into helping form what had been known in the Thirties and Forties as a front organization—but a front for what?

Now, to be clear, at this point in my life, 1987, whatever schoolboy romance that Marxism held for me had long disappeared down the ideo-logical drain. I had no interest in forming a front of any sort or being a shill for its formation, yet I had my own reasons for engaging with, indeed, helping to develop, this organization, not the least of which was basic self-interest. I knew it would be good for my career, doling out trips to foreign ports to writer friends on the one hand while alluding to my "KGB connections" in Hollywood meetings on the other. And meeting all these international characters would give me something to write about, feed my delusions about being the next Greene or le Carré, even if I never got to meet those august writers in the flesh. The average

American mystery writer doesn't get to hang out with KGB colonels, real or imagined. And hang out I did, walking along Moscow's Arbat with Semyonov, an experience akin to walking along Carnaby Street with Mick Jagger. He was that well known. Writers have always been greater celebrities in Russia than America. And Philip Roth's thesis on the difference between writers East and West—in the West everything is possible and nothing counts; in the East nothing is possible and everything counts—seemed entirely accurate to me.

But there was something more complex and personal going on for me on the trip. I was, after all, a Russian writer by heritage myself, specifically a Russian Jewish writer. My father's family had come from Odessa and they, the Russians with us, were acutely aware of it. Odessa was, of course, the Ukraine, but such distinctions, as I learned, were only important when they wanted them to be. Ukrainian or Russian, I was one of them—the boy that got away, their American cousin.

This was very much in the air when I first met the leaders of the IACW's Russian branch in Moscow—the Weiner Brothers (Arkady and Georgy) and Arkady Wachsberg. The Weiner Brothers were authors, like Semyonov, of hugely popular thrillers, but Wachsberg wasn't even a fiction writer as far as I could tell, though still, for some reason, a member of their branch of the International Association of Crime Writers. I was told he was an "important" constitutional scholar and human rights advocate. But all of them were Jewish (Semyonov was half-Jewish) and treated me like a long-lost relative. Indeed, they even *looked* like my relatives, the equally long gone ones from the Bronx, slightly foul-smelling, in ill-fitting Eastern European clothes. These Muscovites were all close to my age, but seemed a decade or two older and about seventy pounds of bad food heavier. Soviet life was obviously hard on the body. (It was also a place where your ethnicity meant even more than it did in the U.S.; it was right there on your identity card for all to see, ineradicable: Tartar, Jew, Kazakh. Racial profiling wasn't frowned upon. It was legislated.)

I was feeling like a participant in a strange reunion whose purpose I couldn't divine. Visiting Georgy Weiner in his home was like a trip back in time to the Bronx's Grand Concourse of the 1950s, although he and his warm family lived in the relative luxury of the high-rise known as Scriptwriter II, because its tenants had to be screen and television writers, at least for part of their work. The Soviet government obviously liked to keep such types on short leashes, encouraging them to live and dine together, when they could afford it, at the ornate Union of Soviet Writers. Semyonov and Weiner took me to eat sturgeon there in the shadow of Maxim Gorky. Yevgeny Yevtushenko, ur-dissident and author of "Babi Yar," one of the most handsome men I had ever seen, ate at the next table. (He was later revealed to be a party hack and toady for Brezhnev.) The Russian writers were showing off their world to me, but at the same time I sensed that they wanted to flee it, wanted me to help them. But I didn't know how—and they weren't saying that they really wanted it in a forthright manner, anyway. There was more going on than I understood—or understand now for that matter. It's Byzantium for a reason.

This uneasy feeling continued as our entourage moved from Moscow to Yalta on the Black Sea, where the meetings of our organization would take place at the Yalta Hotel. But meetings about what? What was it incumbent on us to decide or do? The other Anglosphere writers—including Simon Brett from the United Kingdom and Eric Wright from Canada—and I discussed this among ourselves continually, but we were never able to come a conclusion. What were we *really* doing there?

These meetings in Yalta would begin quite late, around ten or eleven at night, to give us ample time to digest our dinners, the Russians said. Actually, we were already too exhausted to think, but that was the point. They wanted us too tired to resist them. During the day we had had full schedules, going off in buses on excursions to local sites like Chekhov's house or Semyonov's own quaint mountain cabin (*izba*) where his aged mother awaited us for a formal introduction. She looked just like my Grandma Tillie, born in Odessa, who died when I was a child. Another time we were taken to a much larger wooded retreat where servants out of *The Cherry Orchard* filled our bowls with ladles of a distinctly prerevolutionary pheasant soup. Yet another excursion took us to a Young Pioneer Camp, where children of the *nomenklatura* sang patriotic songs along the shores of the Black Sea.

On the way to and from these appointments, Oleg, my interpreter, would sit next to me on the bus, or just behind me, inquiring how I was enjoying my experience and asking what I'd write about my trip on my return. He would comment on my novels, too, which he'd been reading.

"I am interested in your book *California Roll*," he said. "It is an interesting story of America and Japan, but you know these scenes with the GRU ... " He was referring to Soviet Military intelligence, who, in the story, stage a raid at a Zen monastery in Kyoto. "They would not do that."

"How would *you* know, Oleg?" I replied playfully. He nodded, realizing I was teasing. "I know," he said. No doubt he did. And no doubt the GRU never would have done that. I could have used his advice at an earlier date.

Another time he asked me, out of the blue, whether I had heard of "Comrade Dzerzhinsky."

"Yes, I have," I answered, thinking what an odd thing it was of him to ask. I didn't know *that much* of Felix Dzerzhinsky, but I did know that he was the founder of the Bolshevik secret police wing of the Tsar's Cheka, known for its use of the most extreme torture and summary mass executions. He was nicknamed "Iron Felix" for the giant bronze statue of him that then dominated the square in front of Moscow's Lubyanka Prison and for, I presumed, his general lack of basic human empathy. (That statue was toppled by a cheering crowd in 1991.)

"Did you know Comrade Dzerzhinky was half-Jewish?" he continued, leaning in as if sharing a secret.

"No, Oleg, I didn't," I answered. What was this about? Was the interpreter trying to play some weird form of the race or religion card?

"He is misunderstood, Roger. He was a kind and gentle man who was forced to do what he did for the good of the proletariat."

"Dzerzhinksy?" I said.

"Look." The interpreter reached into his pocket and pulled out an old 35mm camera with the initials FED on the top plate where it might have said Leica or Nikon. "He started a company for orphaned boys to produce these—just so the poor children had some money. Felix Edmondovich Dzerzhinsky. FED." He pointed to the initials. "They still make these cameras today. For the kids."

I didn't know what to say.

Nor did I know what to say during our nightly meetings. Our Russian chapter was making an odd request, asking the rest of us to "command" the Russian branch of our organization into existence. Not only that, they wanted us to "command" them to publish a magazine—*Detective.*

This made no sense to us. How could we do that, even if we wanted to? We had no official standing ourselves, we told the Russians. And who would pay for this magazine and pay its contributors who were to come from across the world? But that capitalistic question didn't seem to matter to the Russians, who kept insisting they wanted us to "command" them. They were playing by a rule book none of us foreign devils understood. In fact, it made us very uneasy, although, in retrospect—indeed, to some degree even then—I realize that they were reaching out to us for help in starting a real business in the midst of their still heavily regulated communist economy. But they had too much pride—and were probably too afraid, as well—to say so directly

Of course, they weren't the only ones who were afraid. We Westerners realized that we were in over our heads. Returning for lunch one day, the other shoe dropped. Marco Tropea, the other Italian publisher, and I were riding up the elevator together when it accidentally opened on the third floor, where none of us had ever gone before. Only a few feet away was our Bulgarian delegate, the one who sang gypsy songs for us at night. His mouth was agape and his face beet-red; he was standing in a room full of listening devices, roughly a dozen reel-to-reel tape recorders attached to lines running haphazardly toward the ceiling like a jumble of piano wires. The Bulgarian himself was clutching a half-unspooled reel of tape.

On the one hand it was like a scene out of the Marx Brothers, and on the other hand, totally frightening. Moments later I was back in my suite with my roommate Simon Brett, standing on the bed and carefully pulling back the painting above the headboard. Behind it was an obvious microphone the size of a silver dollar. Simon and I shook our heads in amazement at the absolutely terrifying obviousness of it all as I gingerly let the painting fall back in place. Then I went and wrote the words "What could they possibly want from us?" on a hotel scratch pad. He raised his hands in bewilderment. I went downstairs again to find Paco and complain to him. "So what should we do?" I said. "There is nothing we can do," he replied. "That's the way they are. They do it to Julian, too, I'm sure."

Against that atmosphere and that very evening, Oleg said, "Excuse me, Roger. But do you know what it is *Soviet Screen*?" I nodded. It was a movie magazine. "There is a woman here from this publication. She would like to interview you. If you do not mind … " Not knowing what to expect, and pretty exasperated at this point, I followed him into a waiting room. "This is Mrs. Lieberman," he said, gesturing ahead of him before abruptly leaving, shutting the door behind him.

A woman of perhaps twenty-five got up from the couch and walked over to me. She was attractive, but in a distinctly ethnic Jewish manner you don't often see in the States anymore, not since the advent of ubiquitous nose jobs in the Sixties.

"How do you do, Mr. Simon?" She smiled broadly and extended her hand—and held mine in hers for longer than I expected. Although she'd been introduced as "Mrs.," there was no wedding ring on her finger. "I hope you do not mind an interview. We do not have many visitors from Hollywood and the readers of *Soviet Screen* would be very interested in your opinions." She gestured to the couch and I sat down. Instead of taking a seat across from me, she sat beside me, almost touching. For a moment she was silent, just smiling at me. "How can we help you?" she said finally. "Help me?" I asked. "Yes, how can we help you at *Soviet Screen*? With your career … "

I was already tense, but now I was starting to feel *very* tense. "I don't understand. I thought this was interview—you were going to ask me questions."

"Yes, we would like to help you. We would like to see you do well in your business, Roger." She took out a cigarette and held it up for me to light. "You are our friend." She was staring at me now with a look that I recognized more from movies than from real life. I also noticed that her hand was trembling ever so slightly. I wasn't the only one who was nervous. Of course, the whole moment was awkward beyond words—and not just because I didn't smoke, had no match, and couldn't take her out of her misery by lighting the cigarette. "This evening, you might want to go dancing?" she asked.

"I, uh … " Now all I could think of was the bank of tape recorders and wondered where the microphone in that room was hidden. Maybe there was a video camera.

"We hope you have enjoyed your visit to the Soviet Union." She leaned in closer, touching my sleeve. "Some people here would like to make an arrangement with you. We could help you, if you help us."

That was the last thing I heard from her because I stood up at that point and half ran, half stumbled out of the room without looking back. The only thing in my mind at that moment was how soon I was going to get out of Russia.

And that I did, on schedule, about two days later. Why would they want to recruit me, I kept thinking on the long flight home? What could they possibly want or get from me? In retrospect, I suspect it's simply what they do—they cast a net and see who they can bring in. Who knows? If they'd succeeded, I might have been able to get them the inside dope on the real attitudes behind the pronouncements of the latest left-leaning movie star. Or more likely I could give information about more obscure people, what screenwriter may or may not have been sympathetic to socialism, just as was done in the Thirties and Forties by the playwright John Howard Lawson.

Not that I ever would have dreamed of doing such a thing. They had completely misjudged me, which clearly showed how unsophisticated they really were. The more time I spent in the Soviet Union, the more I despised, more precisely dreaded, them and their culture. I was smart enough to see that there was little difference between the Tsar's Cheka (authors of *The Protocols of the Elders of Zion*) and Dzerzhinsky's nascent NKVD into KGB, just as there is little between the KGB and today's SVR (Foreign Intelligence Service) under Putin. Perhaps I didn't know then the famous Russian saying, "There's no such thing as an ex-Chekist," but I certainly sensed it. Finally getting out of the Soviet Union that time felt like being released from jail.

I wrote about my Soviet experiences in a humorous essay for the *New York Times Book Review* that September called "My Week With Oleg 1: Writers, Detectives, and the Caviar Mafia." Although I did make wry mention of the heavy presence of spies, I decided to leave out my encounter with "Mrs. Lieberman." Part of the reason was that I wasn't *absolutely* certain she was trying to draft me for Soviet intelligence (perhaps it was just my intense paranoia, but what else could it have been?) but the larger reason was that I wanted to give the International Association of Crime Writers a chance. I didn't want it to come crashing down as a front organization, although it was one, in part.

Was that self-interest? Yes. I *was* now the North American Vice-President. But also I suspected a writers' organization with officers on both sides of the Iron Curtain was on balance a good thing at that point in history. Further, who would have wanted to write a piece skeptical of *glasnost* for the *New York Times* then? I doubt they would have published it. Also, in those days, I lived in fear of the *New York Times*, and what they'd say about my next book or movie, over which they had far too much power. Consciously or unconsciously, I wanted to curry favor with them. No more.

As it turned out, the IACW lasted—in fact, it still exists long past the era in which it could have served as a front—and it has been a useful, though scarcely revolutionary, international writers organization, giving out prizes and encouraging translations, the kinds of things literary groups do. But what it did for me was to cement my relations with Julian Semyonov and Paco Taibo and to expand my horizons. I went off to other meetings of the organization, principally in Gijon, Spain, where Paco had organized the Semana Negra (Black Week)—an annual celebration of crime writers where the usual repetitive panel discussions about the genre—endless replies to Edmund Wilson's "Who Cares Who Killed Roger Ackroyd?"—were spiced up with roller coaster rides and costumed Asturian peasant dances with odd-looking instruments resembling bagpipes. I was El Presidente of this event one year and got to help pick the other "delegados," making me a source of free plane tickets and paella for such esteemed mystery writers as Martin Cruz Smith, Ross Thomas, and Donald Westlake. It was kind of like being a low-rent Soviet apparatchik.

But far more interesting and ultimately instructive was when my foreign crime writer friends came to visit me in Hollywood—most specifically Semyonov. Early in 1990, I drove my KGB colonel buddy around Los Angeles, which he pronounced a beautiful city (many Americans would disagree). I introduced him to the movie biz by taking him to dinner with director Paul Mazursky and screenwriter David Freeman at Musso & Frank—the venerable Hollywood restaurant where Fitzgerald, Faulkner, and Chandler supposedly played poker in the back room.

Another time I escorted him onto the studio lot at Disney. Semyonov fit right in. He was a "player," if there ever was one, and a player with experiences more bloody even than Hollywood deal making. He could eat the most venal Hollywood player for lunch, when it came down to it. But I sensed too that the KGB colonel and best-selling Russian felt inferior, that visiting in the U.S. gave him the uneasy sensation that life had passed him by. Sometimes he became very moody and would express this in odd ways. He confessed to me that what he was most envious of in America was our ability to use credit cards. He repeated this to me several times. As high as he was in the nomenklatura, he had to travel abroad with cash only. I think that was his way of acknowledging that with all the power he had, he was not really free.

He was actually in California on his way to Nicaragua to visit with the Sandinista. He invited me to come. I demurred, but through Julian I met one of the better known Sandinistas, Omar Cabezas, their Minister of Culture and the author of *Fire from the Mountain*, the personal account of his days as a guerilla fighting Somoza, the Nicaraguan dictator. While it wasn't a best-seller, there was quite a buzz around the book in left-wing circles. Omar was en route from Paris where he had done some readings and was heading on to Managua with Julian. Cabezas arrived at my house late one night, a glamorous, almost Che-like figure in a goatee and one of those green Sandinista berets. Omar's reputation as a ladies' man preceded him and it was easy to see where it came from. He didn't have a hotel and I offered to put him up—he and Julian were bound for Nicaragua the next morning.

We sat up drinking for a bit. He signed a book to me, made one last invitation for me to go to Nicaragua with them, and then we all went to bed. I was thinking maybe I *should* go. I was single then. My marriage with Renee was long over. In some ways it had hardly ever started. What other chance would I have for such an adventure? I was promised a chance to meet Daniel Ortega, leader of the Sandinista revolution. (This was years before the repellent allegations of child abuse against him.) But then I fell off to sleep. I slept longer than I anticipated—I imagine because I really didn't feel like heading off with them—and could hear Julian and Cabezas rummaging around in the morning. I stumbled out the front door in my pajamas to shake their hands just as they got into a cab for the airport.

Then, feeling a bit wan and cowardly, I walked back into the kitchen for some coffee. Gioconda, my three-day-a-week housekeeper, stood there, white as a sheet and with trembling hands. She was a very sweet woman with polite young children, and I had never seen her like this. "What's wrong, Gioconda?" I asked her in Spanish. She spoke no English. But all she could muster in reply was "Don Rojer..." before looking down. She always called me "Don," despite my protestations. Eventually, I admit, I enjoyed its Cervantean formality. No one had ever treated me in such a courtly manner. But now I could see she was really disturbed. She was looking down in a way that I also had never seen and appeared to be near tears.

"What's wrong?" I repeated. She didn't answer immediately. Finally, she said, "I recognized that man in your house." There was tremendous disappointment in her voice, as if I had betrayed her in some way. Then I realized—how stupid of me! Gioconda was Nicaraguan. "Omar Cabezas?" I said. "Yes, Sandinista," Gioconda intoned, moving her head up and down in staccato motion as if trying to catch her breath. "They shot my family in Leon. They are murderers."

I didn't know what to say.

A year or so later I was back for a second time in the Soviet Union, but not at the behest of the International Association of Crime Writers. I was with a delegation of screenwriters from the Writers Guild of America. This was an A-list group including William Goldman (*All the President's Men*), Larry Kasdan (*The Big Chill*), Paul Schrader (*Taxi Driver*), and Julius Epstein (the fairly aged co-screenwriter of *Casablanca*). I suppose I made this august group because I was hot at the time off of *Enemies, A Love Story*.

None of them had been to the Soviet Union before and, to my surprise, didn't seem to have much knowledge of it or—for that matter, if truth be told—much curiosity. When we were offered the chance to hear the then renegade Boris Yeltsin speak at their Cinematographer's Union, I was the only one who wanted to go. And I did, hanging on my interpreter's every word. The event was quite dramatic, like being at a revolutionary meeting from an earlier epoch, because the Cinematographer's Union was at the cutting edge of *glasnost*, which had progressed quite far from my previous visit and was almost ready to burst open to democracy under the eager, if sadly unstable, leadership of the seemingly good-hearted Yeltsin. When I got back, I waxed enthusiastic about the event to my colleagues who, to my amazement, seemed completely uninterested. They were too busy talking to each other.

Looking back, this blasé attitude of my Hollywood brethren toward this positive political change could be seen as a harbinger of Hollywood's strangely cocoon-like reaction to 9/11, when, after a brief interlude, the rise of radical Islam was regarded as an inconvenient blip in the pervasive cloud of political correctness. Despite their trendy image, most Hollywood people don't like change. They want things as they are.

What did interest the writers on our trip, not surprisingly, were the screenings of their own movies, which were welcomed by the culturally starved Soviet audiences. People like Kasdan and Goldman had written mega-hits (*Indiana Jones* and *Butch Cassidy*) that were previously unknown to them. The only movie authored by one of our company that was familiar to all the Russians, Ukrainians, and even Georgians we met (Tblisi, its capital, was a stop on our trip), was *Casablanca*. Its co-author— Julius Epstein, an appealing, gnomish man who resembled E. T.—was a hero to them, feted everywhere he went with the traditional communist red roses.

Of course, the audience wasn't really communist anymore. When introduced at our stage presentation in Tblisi, I undiplomatically stated that I hoped we'd be returning to a "free and independent Georgia soon." I made a kind of shortened revolutionary fist and saw my colleagues frown at my grandstanding, but the audience broke out in the most spontaneous round of applause I had ever had and probably ever will. I felt great. This was undoubtedly the nascent pro-American me that would burst forth publicly after 9/11.

An earlier version of that me had popped out on my previous crime writer trip to the Soviet Union under not entirely dissimilar circumstances. Our group of largely leftist mystery writers was squired to a decrepit theater in downtown Yalta, where we stood in front of an audience of locals "interested in culture." Each of us was grandly introduced as if he was an avatar of Dickens or Melville, and Semyonov asked for questions. There was silence. These were the early days of *glasnost* and the Soviet people were still uneasy about speaking in public.

Finally, one elderly vet with a chest full of medals stepped forward and addressed me, the sole American on the stage. "All our people love and respect our General Secretary Gorbachev," his raspy words were translated. "Can you say the same of your President Reagan?" For a moment I didn't know how to respond. "You don't have to answer that," said Semyenov, knowing my politics and that I didn't much care for Reagan then.

But I waved him off and gestured to my interpreter, before taking a step forward. "I disagree with the policies of President Reagan," I said. "But the United States is a democracy. I didn't vote for him. I voted for his opponent." I could hear puzzled, almost anxious muttering in the audience as my civics lesson was translated. "Good answer," said Semyonov, giving me a thumb's up. I could tell he was being sincere. KGB colonel or not, it was hard not to like the guy.

One of the reasons I accepted my second invitation to the Soviet Union with the Writers' Guild group was that it would be a chance to see him again, as well as my other friends in Scriptwriter II. The trip had been arranged on the Soviet end by a Russian screenwriter named Masha Zereva, whom I suspected was burnishing her American connections should she, at some point, want a way out. Masha became a friend of mine, too. Somehow I felt closer to the Russians I was visiting than to the American screenwriters with whom I was traveling. Some of that was an outgrowth of the intense competitiveness of Hollywood, where people's very beings are defined by their credits, but it also was a matter of blood. As I mentioned, on my first visit, Semyonov and the whole Novosti crew (and Oleg, of course) knew of my background in Odessa, the legendary home of artists like Heifetz and Babel, not to mention the Jewish gangsters that were the fodder for Babel's masterpieces. "Ah, you are from Odessa," people would say, meaning you were either a great scoundrel or great artist or both. In fact, the Novosti people offered me a trip to the Black Sea port of my ancestors. I didn't have the time. And by then I didn't have the inclination. But from the first moment I was in Russia on my first visit, I felt as if I had come home, even if that home was a jail the size of a continent.

So I was looking forward to seeing Julian when I returned with the screenwriters. I knew he would be amused by the company I was keeping, because in those days I was living with Pamela Fong, a Chinese-American former Miss Los Angeles. Her father was Benson Fong, the original Number One Son from the Charlie Chan movies. Pamela, however, was too smart to be gulled by the Hollywood glitz and kept her distance, maturing into a serious photographer who did a photographic book of victims of child abuse. But she was still gorgeous, which made me the odd man out on the screenwriters' trip—I was the only one traveling with a "woman not my wife" and the only one, Masha Zereva confided in me, accompanied by a woman who impressed the Russians, who had expected more from Hollywood.

It was clear that Semyonov was similarly impressed when he took Pamela and me to dinner our second night in Moscow. We went to an Azerbaijani restaurant on a gated street that fairly screamed high-level *nomenklatura*. Khruschev, I was told, had lived in one of the villas. The restaurant was part nightclub, the way many Russian places are now in Los Angeles and Brooklyn, with vodka bottles on long tables pointing toward a stage with, in this case, an Azerbaijani orchestra and a woman cranking out a Soviet version of "La Vie En Rose." We sat there knocking down vodka and gossiping about writer friends like Paco, who had bought some upscale digs in Mexico City's Colonia Condesa. I joked that he had made the money from Cuban intelligence, but we knew his detective novels sold like hotcakes in Mexico—although nowhere near Julian's numbers, which were closer to the Harry Potter range.

All the while the Soviet writer stared at Pamela. Julian looked older now and even fatter than when I'd last seen him, but his spirits were good and his energy high as usual. I wanted to introduce him to the other screenwriters in our group. He was interested, but I didn't press it. I knew they wouldn't be interested in him. He promised to take us on an excursion to his dacha (he had another one near Moscow) when we got back to the capital. Our tour was taking us to Leningrad on the night train, where babushka ladies wake you up with tea at dawn, and then by air to Tblisi on a plane with livestock in the aisles, even a goose under a woman's arms. We would be back in a week and Julian would whisk us away for the weekend he promised.

It never happened. When we got back to Moscow, those seven or so days later, I couldn't reach him. After a couple of calls I found out he was in the hospital. I enquired about visiting but was told it wasn't possible. On my way out of Russia, I learned he had died of a coronary.

About a decade later, in January 2003, I was standing in my kitchen when my phone rang. It was Masha Zereva calling from Moscow. After all this time, the Soviet ... now Russian ... screenwriter, with whom I'd had no interim contact, was inviting me to return to her country, this time to be a juror at a film festival in Khanty-Mansisk, Siberia.

"I am telling everyone it is their chance to go to Siberia and to come back," Masha joked. Not surprisingly, I'd never heard of Khanty-Mansisk, but I was certainly intrigued by a *round*-trip to Siberia. I was married again, for my third time, to the screenwriter Sheryl Longin, and we had a then four-year-old daughter Madeleine. I hated to leave them, but this was an offer I couldn't easily refuse, especially since they added a five-thousand-dollar honorarium and business class travel.

Of course, as with all things Russian, that turned out to be more complicated than it sounded. I was to fly with the Russian director Sergei Bodrov, who would be on the jury with me, but lived, of all places, on a ranch south of Tucson. A visa would be sent to me with the tickets from the Embassy of the Russian Republic in San Francisco. Two days before my departure, neither had arrived. A call to the Embassy revealed that they had never heard of me. And even so it would be impossible to get me the visa in time because I would have to ship them my passport with various specifically signed photos and various validated documents with seals I could never get in time. All this was barked out at me by an official who sounded like a particularly bored ex-commissar from a road show version of *Darkness at Noon*. A flurry of last-minute calls to Moscow and FedEx, however, saved the day and soon enough I was seated next to my new friend Sergei Bodrov on an Aeroflot jet from LAX to Sheremetyevo.

While not on the level of Semyonov, Sergei, it turned out, was quite a well-known fellow in Russia as well. An engaging, intelligent man with a stammer, he had directed a film called *Prisoner on the Mountain*, which had been nominated for the Best Foreign Language Film Academy Award in 1996. More importantly and sadly, I would find out on the long flight, he had had a very recent personal tragedy. Sergei's son and star of *Prisoner*, Sergei Bodrov, Jr.—a film director in his own right and something of a Russian national celebrity—had died in an avalanche in the mountains of the North Caucasus only a few months before while shooting his latest film. He was thirty-one. Sergei was going back to Russia to serve on the jury, but also to console his daughter-in-law and, it was apparent, himself. I could see the pain of this horrible event in Sergei's eyes. Within an hour or so of meeting him, it was clear that he was struggling all the time not to think of the loss of his son.

Many hours later we were in Moscow, riding in the middle of the night in a van from Sheremetyevo International Airport to Domodedovo Airport, an hour away on the opposite side of the city. By my side was my new Russian interpreter, Sonya Ginsburg, a tall Jewish woman, again with the classical nasal protuberance of our race. Was this an avatar of "Mrs. Lieberman"? She talked a mile a minute, welcoming me to Russia, seemingly well aware of my previous visits and that I was a friend of Masha's. Was she about to recruit me as well? The idea flitted through my brain but I rejected it as paranoia on my part. It was February 2003. We were in capitalist Russia. The KGB was gone. Still, why were these people always trying to put me together with Jewish women? Was this their idea of a dating service? I was a married man—and happily.

We arrived at Domodedovo, which is the gateway airport to Asia. Hundreds of passengers, many with Mongolian or Kazakh features, milled about a vast hall, waiting for flights that appeared to be greatly delayed, most likely perpetually so. There we met the other jurors— Polish director Krystof Zanussi, Italian producer Rosanna Seregni and German critic Klaus Eder—plus the festival honoree, French comedian Pierre Richard, the star of *The Tall Blond Man with One Black Shoe*. (Every film festival, it seems, needs some kind of honoree, but the aging Richard wasn't exactly Robert Redford level.)

After a continued long delay, we got on our plane to Khanty-Mansisk where we arrived a couple of hours later to be greeted by a choir of locals in regional dresses, some of whom looked Eskimo but I learned were Khants and Mansi people, true Siberians, serenading us with their music. It was four o'clock in the morning their time (who knows what time it was for me?) and they had waited up for us. They had also kept on the multicolored lights that illuminated the snow statues sprinkled through a quaint and lovely town of tiny pastel houses, Disney characters mixed with scenes from Chekhov and the socialist realist logo of MosFilm—the new and old Russia meets Dartmouth Winter Carnival. And winter it was, at least to me—the thermometer read minus ten Fahrenheit, which I was told was something of a heat wave for Siberia in January.

It also stayed pitch dark until ten in the morning, with the sun setting again at two in the afternoon, which soon had my already jetlagged head turned upside down. Ambien (taken to correct jetlag) and the ubiquitous vodka only exacerbated the situation. The large lounge where the festival-goers—mostly Eastern European filmmakers and cineastes, but also some from Western Europe and a few from the States—met had long tables of Russia's favorite beverage lined up in seemingly endless rows of shot glasses, which were instantly replenished as soon as consumed, as if on an assembly line. I downed more than my share, making me alternately depressed and euphoric, like a character from a Russian novel.

This took place during the run-up to the Iraq War. I stumbled around in my besotted state, arguing in favor of the invasion, more often than not getting a stunned reaction, especially from the Western Europeans and those few other Americans. How could I hold such an opinion? The Eastern Europeans had far more complex reactions, having recently seen totalitarianism up close. Many of them supported my view, although with lowered voices or in complete confidence. It was hardly a popular opinion even then in the film world and even in Siberia.

That same Siberian film world, though practically as far as one could get from the movie mainstream, aspired mightily to be part of it. They provided a klieg-lit red carpet for the VIP guests in front of the main theater, many of them luminaries from the Moscow film industry who wore luxurious sable and mink coats and arrived in their car of choice—shiny new black Ford Explorers. Paparazzi shadowed their every move. Several of us began calling it Cannes-Mansisk instead of Khanty-Mansisk.

In actuality the event was called the "Spirit of Fire Festival," and each of us were given spiffy red down parkas emblazoned with its logo, a Siberian shaman extending a fiery torch through film sprockets. The event, which was being held in the newly wealthy oil and lumber region of Western Siberia, had a nouveau riche quality. Conspicuous consumption was everywhere. They took us jurors for frozen picnics of Beluga caviar, reindeer and dog sledding, jet and cross country skiing on an Olympic biathlon course, and on the oil barons' deluxe leather-seated helicopter for a flight over the *taiga* (the coniferous forest, made legendary by Chekhov, that extends across sub-arctic Russia).

Staring down from the helicopter, the expanse was awe-inspiring. I had been told the region was ripe for ecological disaster, but I saw little of that. What I did see was an unlimited snowscape, punctuated every ten or so kilometers by a single human being, trudging ant-like across the whiteness or seated in front of a hole in a field of ice, apparently fishing. I'd never seen anything so barren or so beautiful. Or so lonely. When, after an hour or so, some of the small wooden buildings of the gulag were pointed out to us, I was startled.

"This is where Trotsky was in prison," Sonya Ginsburg explained to me. "You know what it is the gulag?" Yes, I know, I know, I told her. The interpreter had been glued to my side on almost every occasion, except when we were viewing movies or I returned to my room to go to sleep. Sometimes, I'd pretend to go to my room and then sneak back into the main lounge to enjoy the socializing without her accompanying me. The second time I did this, she caught me. "Listen, most of these people speak English so I don't need an interpreter," I told her, as gently as I could. "Besides, I speak French and Spanish."

The truth was that I would do anything to escape her. And not because I feared she was the KGB or its modern equivalent. She was the furthest thing from "Mrs. Lieberman," telling me all the time instead of her relatives in the San Fernando Valley and implying that she'd like nothing more than to join them, if only the right person would take her away from the blight of Russia, pre- or post-Soviet. I was in the midst of a lonely-hearts club for unmarried Russian Jewish women.

"He escaped from there *on foot*," Ginsburg continued, sounding impressed as she nodded out the helicopter window. She referred to Trotsky, whose isolated gulag redoubt we'd just passed over. Indeed it was hard to conceive of anyone making that trek on his own. Whatever else you could say about him, Leon Trotsky, né Lev Bronstein, was one tough character. "This is a hard place," Sonya Ginsburg then said, her voice suddenly noticeably lower, almost a whisper. "Be very careful or they will not pay you." For a moment I didn't know what she was talking about. She must have noticed, because she added in a voice lower still, now barely audible above the whir of the helicopter blades, "You are supposed to get five thousand dollars for serving on jury, no?"

Indeed, I was. And that service was somewhat more onerous than I'd expected, although not nearly so bad that it really merited five thousand dollars for a week's pay, especially since they had flown me from LA to Siberia, put me up in deluxe hotels, and ferried me around like a VIP. All I had to do was watch movies. Of course, they weren't very good movies. For the most part they were deadly dull, including one interminable film from Kazakhstan that purported to tell the Buddha story in reverse.

It lasted over four hours, and I don't think any of us were awake at the end. Most of the others weren't much better.

Only two films were palatable—and perhaps only by comparison—*Year of the Devil,* a Czech rock opera, and *Mostly Martha,* a German melodrama about a woman chef that had already played in the States. We had to choose between these two so-so films for the first-prize Golden Taiga, which had a munificent sum of $150,000 attached to it (to be used, presumably, to jump start the director's next film). The problem was the pressure was being put on us by the Russians to give the award to one of their films, *Black Ice,* a tacky low-rent thriller in the style of a Seventies blaxploitation flick gone Eastern Euro. It was set in 2002's newly trendy Moscow, with oodles of cocaine and already out-of-date techno music. But this was the first "Spirit of Fire" festival and the Russians clearly wanted the first prize for one of their own, all the more so because the director was the son of someone important in their industry.

These Olympics-style pressure tactics disconcerted those of us on the jury and I raised this with local boy Sergei Bodrov, who urged me to compromise and recommend a third prize for the young Russian director, even if his film was, as Sergei well knew, worthless. It would be a good way, he added, to be certain that we'd get our five thousand dollar honoraria (he implied that he'd be included in this). He also recommended we raise the issue with Masha Zereva.

Masha was relieved by the proposed compromise—she was clearly getting pressure of her own from above—and assured the jurors that we'd receive our checks in the mail when we returned to our countries. "Don't do it," Sergei quickly advised me in another low voice. "They will never send it. This is R-R-Russia," he added with his stammer. "Ask for it n-n-now." So, getting a bit Russian myself, I asked that it be given to me immediately, as did several others. The Russians agreed to this, but the problem was, Masha warned, that it was illegal to take more than a hundred dollars in cash out of the Russian Republic, and they checked at customs.

Throwing caution to the wind, I asked for mine, anyway. Sure enough, the next day, just after the awards ceremony and before the final caviar and vodka party at which the young Russian director thanked me profusely for my support of his fine film, I was handed a stack of fifty crisp, new one hundred dollar bills. I had no idea whether they were counterfeit, but it certainly occurred to me that they might be. It also occurred to me that they were the product of some Russian mafia laundry. Who knew?

By the next night I was ensconced in a suite at Moscow's historic though tatty Metropole Hotel near the Kremlin. I was on the lavish VIP floor, unique in that it had its own small museum commemorating the former guests of that floor, among them Lenin, Mao, Trotsky, Zhou Enlai, and Bertolt Brecht. I got the shivers, wondering whose suite I was in. But I was considerably more concerned with what I'd do at the Sheremetyevo Airport customs the next afternoon with the stack of fifty one hundred dollar bills burning a hole in my pocket. Hiding them someplace in my suitcase didn't seem like a good idea. These officials had seen everything, and they were likely to be the same autocratic crew from Soviet days with the same suspicious-bordering-on-paranoid outlook. Russia was the world's capital of *plus ça change*.

I had a plan. With the collaboration of Sonya Ginsburg (not her real name, as you may have surmised by now) I went early the next morning to the Moscow American Express office. There, with the help of my Gold Card, I turned the fifty one hundred dollar bills into five one thousand dollar American Express checks. No questions were asked. I figured that if they were discovered at the airport, I could feign ignorance. These were checks and not cash. Still, it was a risk. As I well knew, the check numbers would be traceable as purchased in Russia, undoubtedly for cash. I was laundering my own money. Oh, well, I thought—the worst that could happen would be that the checks were confiscated. Or was it? Visions of the gulag from the helicopter went through my head.

Of course, things had changed, I told myself repeatedly as I headed to the airport with Sonya Ginsburg. I am grateful that she was my willing accomplice in all this but to this day I am not sure why she was. Perhaps it was those dreams of the San Fernando Valley. I can't say that I blame her.

At Sheremetyevo, because of my "pre-approved" status as a festival juror, I seemed to have no choice but to use the VIP entrance. Also, Sonya Ginsburg insisted that any attempt not to use this privilege would be a—pardon the expression—red flag. So I had to cool my heels in apparent aristocratic pleasure in a small lounge where I was plied with endless rounds of tea I didn't want from an ornate samovar. Only a few feet away was my personal customs officer, a stocky female former commissar-type who looked like a refugee from a casting call for *From Russia, With Love*. I wanted nothing more than to get past her to the door just behind, which led to the freedom of the duty free shops, where I fully intended to dispose of a solid portion of my hidden checks as quickly as possible on gifts for friends and family.

Doing my best not to tap my foot, I watched Sonya for her unspoken acknowledgment that the time was ripe for me to go forward. I didn't get one and finally took the bull by the horns and walked directly to the customs lady who looked surprised that I was attempting to leave so early. Forcing the apprehensive Sonya into translating, I told her I would like to go through now to use the duty free store. "Do you have anything to declare?" the lady replied, staring at me with cold expression of one who expects everybody to be lying—and indeed I was.

She asked, "Do you have any currency?" I quickly took a fistful of crumpled bills out of my pocket. "Just a few hundred rubles. I intend to use them to buy a present for my daughter." I gestured toward the shops, adding the half-truth to protect my lie. The official scarcely batted an eye. It was obvious that she never believed anybody about anything. She glanced over at Sonya, as if to emphasize her skepticism. But then, without a word, she waved me through. I did my best not to run.

Back in LA, I presented to my wife and daughter two of those beautiful Russian fur hats that so attract the enmity of PETA on Fifth Avenue. As residents of Southern California, to this day they have never worn them. But Madeleine is the proud possessor of what I would assume to be one of the most extensive collection of Russian nesting dolls between Port Hueneme and the Mexican border, compliments of the first "Spirit of Fire" film festival. Some of them are quite beautiful, almost museum pieces.

But it doesn't end there. Several months later—either because of my blog, where I had written about the festival or because of an article I had written about it for the *Los Angeles Times*—I was contacted via email by one of the producers of *Year of the Devil*, the Czech film that had won the Golden Taiga. As of then, they had not received one penny of the $150,000 promised for the award. They wondered if I would be able to help them. Although I knew the chances of this were between slim and none, I fired off some emails to the relevant addresses I had. Not surprisingly, I heard nothing. After all, it was, as Sergei Bodrov said, "R-R-Russia."

I stayed friends with Sergei, who didn't live, as I noted, in his native land but on a ranch south of Tucson with his American wife, at least when he wasn't making a movie. Eventually that marriage broke up and I lost contact with the Russian director until he turned up in Los Angeles at the very moment I was writing the Russian chapter of this book. That bit of serendipity was caused by Bodrov having been nominated for his second Best Foreign Language Film Academy Award, a feat performed only by people with names like Fellini and De Sica. The nominated picture was *Mongol*—an ambitious, surprisingly positive biopic about Genghis Khan, directed in the epic style of Ford and Kurosawa.

I had lunch with him at a restaurant in West Hollywood in the run-up to the 2008 Oscars. He had aged only slightly, despite having spent the last four years working on his movie in godforsaken locations from Outer Mongolia to Kazakhstan. Much of the talent had yet to be paid, although the film was nominated for an Academy Award. It sounded like the typical independent movie story and then some.

We reminisced about Khanty-Mansisk. I told him of my email from the producer of the prize-winning film, wondering where his money was. Sergei got defensive about his motherland. It was the same with the Czechs, he insisted. When he was awarded a $25,000 prize at Karlovy Vary for *Prisoner of the Mountain*, he had to beg them for his money for six months.

Still, that didn't prevent him from lamenting the current state of Khanty-Mansisk, where he had been recently. Gone was the small village with the pastel houses. "It's all K-K-KGB now," he told me, referring of course to the world of Putin and his cronies. "They live in big new chalets like your M-M-McMansions. It's so cynical, Roger. In old days, so optimistic." He meant 2003.

"And Masha Zereva?" I asked. She and her husband Pavel were doing very well, he assured me with a wry smile. Their daughter had married a Russian oil baron and they had a villa in Nice. From a tiny apartment in Scriptwriter II to the French Riviera, I thought—in less than half a decade! And I'd worried about Masha escaping communism. "She is smart Russian J-J-Jewish lady," Sergei reminded me. I didn't need to be told.

I wished Sergei luck with the Oscar, though I suspected he wouldn't win it. Perhaps that was the Russian Jew in me as well, a hint of darkness. I wondered about my DNA as I drove home from lunch. I'd learned things on my three excursions to his country, but most of all the visits may have made me a little bit tougher, a little more cynical. Russia tended to do that to people. In my case, I wasn't sure if that was a good or bad thing.

8 EVOLUTION: THE BIRTH OF AN ACCIDENTAL ONLINE APOSTATE CEO

The man Sergei met in the West Hollywood restaurant that winter day in 2008 was not the same man who'd accompanied him to Siberia just five years before. I certainly wasn't the same man who'd walked down Moscow's Arbat with Julian Semyonov or hobnobbed with Regis Debray in the corridors of Havana's Hotel Nacional. No, I had turned into someone I would likely have despised as a young man.

Certainly a lot of other people now despised me. I was attacked on a daily basis on websites across the world, reviled by people who once had adored—or at least admired—me, and received more hate mail than I ever could have imagined. I also felt ostracized to one degree or another by the Hollywood community in which I'd made my life. Of course, I had many new friends, bedfellows I never would have conceived in my wildest imagination, some with names I myself had been reviling for years. Yes, they turned out to be people, too. And all this happened—at least in part—by accident.

In the spring of 2003 I was about to have a novel published, *Director's Cut*, the eighth in the Moses Wine series. Its subject matter, terrorism on a Prague movie set, and point of view reflected my—and Moses Wine's—political migration away from the Left. (The book begins, a tad tongue-in-cheek, "I knew I was in trouble when I was starting to agree with John Ashcroft....") Not just because of this shift, I suspected that my publisher, Atria Books of Simon & Schuster, wasn't going to do much to promote it. And in discussions with them, they didn't give me much reassurance to allay my suspicions. It also had been a long time again since the last of the Wine books and I wondered if my fan base would still be there—and, if so, whether they would feel betrayed by the "New Moses."

What to do?

Like many people, after 9/11 I had gone online to try to make sense of the cataclysm. In the process, I discovered blogs—principally Instapundit, the home of a Tennessee law professor named Glenn Reynolds, and Little Green Footballs, the idiosyncratic product of web designer Charles Johnson. Johnson, a refugee from the music world as I was from film, and once a sideman for pianist Al Jarreau and bassist Stanley Clarke, was evidently undergoing a political transformation similar to mine. I had determined that the usual author websites were static affairs—little more than digital brochures—that few would want to visit. Why not create a blog, I thought, like Reynolds and Johnson, to promote my forthcoming novel? (The form probably intrigued me as well.) I contacted Johnson and asked him to design a blog for me. As it turned out, he was a fan of *The Big Fix*, and he was pleased to do it.

Soon enough I was online and blogging. It was surprisingly liberating. After decades of listening to editors, publishers, producers, actors, directors, movie executives—everyone, as the writer-producer Jay Allen once told me, from the elevator operator to the head of the studio—I was on my own. I was the publishing house, and, to my amazement, the publishing house took off, in a small way, at any rate. In short order, thanks in large to degree to be being linked by Glenn Reynolds and to a smaller degree to the fact that, unlike most bloggers, I was not an entirely unknown writer, the blog rose quickly in popularity. I would have as many as twenty thousand readers online in one day, heady stuff for an author rarely lucky enough to sell that many books in hardcover over the course of a year. Unfortunately, however, this newfound popularity did little for my immediate intention—to promote my novel. Perhaps I'd gone online too late, with too little lead-time for my March 2003 publication date.

In any case, most of my new readers couldn't have cared less about crime fiction. These people were coming for my political opinions, some of which I was just discovering for myself, revealing them on the Internet almost at the moment of their conception. It was an exhilarating interactive experience that I shared with others online. Instead of reading pundits, I was one. And apparently—this should have been no shock, but it was—I wasn't the only person undergoing the equivalent of a political sex-change operation at that moment. There were plenty of others under that knife in the aftermath of the World Trade Center.

Many of them faced the same problems I did, friends and family turning away, employment issues, and so forth. Some of these new apostates were psychotherapists and psychiatrists blogging under names like Neo-neocon, Shrinkwrapped, and Dr. Sanity. Others were from the literary world, like the former book and magazine editor Gerard Vanderleun. They were as alienated from peers in their professions as I was from mine. I was also in contact with three brilliant fellow Dartmouth alumni—John Hinderaker, Scott Johnson, and Paul Mirengoff—who had established the Powerline blog, which almost immediately gained national respect and a citation for Blog of the Year from *TIME*.

Soon I found myself part of a community that, for the first time in years, extended way beyond Hollywood to places like Barcelona (José Guardia), Tel Aviv (Allison Kaplan Sommer), Sydney (Richard Fernandez), and Baghdad (Omar and Mohammed Fadhil of the influential Iraq the Model blog). Almost without my realizing it, my blog—not screen or fiction writing—had begun to take up most of my writing time.

Meanwhile, I found myself invited to speak at conferences on New Media (whatever that was—I assumed anything that happened online) and to appear on radio as, of all things, a screenwriter as political pundit. The hosts, like Hugh Hewitt of the Salem network or onetime NOW president turned conservative Tammy Bruce, would seek my opinion of what the insider Hollywood view of the latest ideological contretemps was—as if I knew. The truth was I was no longer part of Hollywood to any real extent. I was part of *them*.

But I wasn't making any money out of it. Yes, I made random dollars through advertising and, yes, a few people were hitting the "tip jar" donation button tucked discreetly on the side of the page. But frankly, the latter embarrassed me. I was far too old and had spent far too many years as a professional writer to enjoy being the literary equivalent of a busker in the London Tubes.

Of course, I wasn't the only one thinking that something more substantial had to be made of this new form—and not just for monetary reasons, but to extend our reach and, paradoxically, to formalize this new medium without destroying its spontaneity. The intensity of this desire was increasing because some of the blogs with a more rightward tilt had uncovered the prevarications of CBS anchorman Dan Rather in the matter of the forged Bush National Guard papers. One of the leaders in this was Charles Johnson, who exposed the forgery on his blog by replicating the decades-old papers with a recent version of Microsoft Word, making Rather and his *60 Minutes* producers seem as dishonest as they were politically dumb and procrustean.

Charles and I had been talking about how to expand some of the blogs we knew into a media company. I was also becoming friendlier with Glenn Reynolds, whose wide-ranging intelligence and catholic interests reminded me on a daily basis of how circumscribed my Hollywood experience had been. We consulted with Glenn about our dreamed of blog aggregation. But none of us had much business knowledge. Charles had dabbled in a software company for a bit and I had my years in the movie industry, which were rather more like being on *Survivor* than actually running an enterprise, so we joined up with another blogger, Marc Danziger. Marc had background as a kind of corporate trouble-shooter, so he prepared something I'd never seen before called a PowerPoint presentation, and the two of us headed north to Silicon Valley to raise venture capital for our new company.

Not surprisingly, we didn't get very far. Still coming down from the deflation of the infamous tech bubble, the VC people were not in an expansive mode. And even if they had been, I doubt that they would have known then what to make of our proposed aggregation, with a screenwriter who knew more about plot points than PowerPoint at the helm. The truth is I never felt more of a "fish out of water," to use the cliché for a certain genre of Hollywood movie, than I did on those first visits to Silicon Valley's Sand Hill Road. Now, as the entertainment and tech industries move inexorably closer together, the Valley seems more like a second home.

The truth was at that point there was a rift between Danziger and Charles and me. Charles and I were, as Marc put it, "content guys." He was a systems guy, more interested in the kind of technical Internet strategies you read about in *Wired* like the evolution of the "long tail." From a business point of view, he may have been right. And he was certainly right about the differences between us. Charles and I were and are "content guys." We wanted to revolutionize the content of media, making it more open to a diversity of opinion, more responsive to its readership, and ultimately more responsible to the truth—or at least the search for it.

Glenn Reynolds supported this approach, and his blog Instapundit would become the flagship of the new media company that would be called Pajamas Media. The name came from the Dan Rather affair, when Jonathan Klein, a CBS executive, went on Fox News to dismiss those of us criticizing the anchorman as mere amateurs writing in our pajamas. Evidently, the executive needed to brush up on his Proust—and the numerous other authors who had done some of their best writing in bed. Notwithstanding this exec's cheesy aspersions, Rather lost his job and Pajamas Media is an existing, though still fragile, new media company.

Charles and I finally found much of the money to start the company with a businessman named Aubrey Chernick. Although he lived in a Los Angeles canyon not far from Steven Spielberg and Arnold Schwarzenegger, Aubrey—who had made his money in software—was the furthest thing from an entertainment industry type, at least so it seemed to me when Charles and I first met him. He and his wife Joyce had evenings in their home to which they invited speakers with an interest in the War on Terror, like Daniel Pipes. Charles and I were invited to meet Aubrey at one of these and it was close to midnight before we sat down with the man face-to-face. Because the meeting began so late (I didn't realize what a night owl Aubrey was at that point), I assumed we were on another wild goose chase; but within minutes it became clear that Chernick was seriously interested in helping fund Pajamas Media.

Of course, much time was spent, many I's dotted, and considerable blood spilled before Pajamas Media made its debut in November 2005 under the stuffy corporate name OSM (Open Source Media), a huge blunder made out of the starting gate. Before that, however, I became CEO. Now I could say that that was entirely an accident, but, as one well-known American has said, "that would be a lie."

Somewhere along the line I realized that someone was going to be in charge of the thing. Marc Danziger, who was still with us and always (because of his business experience) saw himself in the role of Chief Executive Office, started to get edgy about the direction we were going in. He also felt that Charles and I were too close, that we might be ganging up on him. We weren't, but it's true that we were friends. It was also true that I was becoming closer to Aubrey. As a business neophyte, I decided to listen to the advice of someone who had been immensely successful in that area, Chernick, as opposed to Marc, who didn't have anything remotely like that kind of track record. Tensions rose as the company approached becoming a reality and Marc, receiving a settlement, withdrew. The board, largely Aubrey, asked me to be CEO.

And then the troubles began.

None of us really knew what to do. New Media, whatever its provenance, is still a business, and we had to organize around business principles, even if we were herding the proverbial cats, ninety (and growing) wildly individualistic bloggers with ideological spread from Michelle Malkin to David Corn of *The Nation*. (Despite our best efforts, Corn and other left-wing bloggers like my old friend the journalist Marc Cooper are not longer with us. It's no surprise that in our time it proved very difficult to keep left and right together.) But what would this mean in practice? How would we preserve the integrity of the blogosphere while evolving into a viable, profit-making enterprise? This is where the blunders began. We decided to hire a branding company, one of those strange institutions that tell you who you are and what you should call yourself. It should be no surprise that I had only vaguely heard of such operations until about a week before we hired one. But a-branding we did go.

When I think back now on the spectacle of Charles Johnson—the aging hippie in his fifties still with a blond pony tail—and me sitting around a conference table in West Hollywood watching a slide show on the "history of names" from the Greeks to Coca-Cola, I have to laugh to preserve my sanity. This exercise took up the first two days of this company's traditional presentation, for which we were paying a hundred thousand dollars (as opposed to reading about it in a book for $19.95). At the time, I felt I had just joined some new form of corporate Scientology. Even after this charade, neither the branding company nor Charles and I could come up with an acceptable name. (*Acme* Media, if you can believe it, was considered—and only half in jest.)

Now, of course, we'd called ourselves Pajamas Media from the outset internally, as well as to the ninety or so bloggers we had assembled. We were aggregating these blogs into a news and opinion plus advertising network. And, yes, we were well aware that the Internet was filled with success stories of companies with goofy names—Yahoo, Google, Amazon, etc. Why not Pajamas? Yet still we thought to choose something more official and corporate sounding, and came up with OSM, or Open Source Media, which was an at best perfunctory bow to our roots.

How wrong we were. In the midst of our fancy, overpriced debut at the W Hotel in New York, replete with press conferences, panel discussions hooked up to Spain and Iraq, cocktail receptions, and a keynote speech by journalist Judith Miller—just emerged from her recent incarceration for refusing to divulge the sources of her *New York Times* stories on Scooter Libby and Valerie Plame—we were informed that a tiny online radio station called Open Source was accusing our new Internet behemoth of plagiarizing its name. The World Wide Web erupted. News of our arrogance sailed to the top of Technorati in number of links, passing even Paris Hilton for a couple of days. The new and presumptuous OSM had taken the name of a poor honest innocent little "netizen" podcaster.

As it turned out, we had done no such thing. The podcaster had no legal claim to Open Source Media. But we were embarrassed. Never mind that much of the criticism came, as it usually does in such circumstances, from envy. Charles and I felt terrible. Everything our critics had said about us was true. We were The Man.

We tried to turn lemons into the proverbial lemonade by going back as quickly as we could to our roots. We publicly apologized and gave the podcaster back his name. We would be Pajamas Media, once again. Indeed, we are Pajamas Media, or PJM, to this day, and now Pajamas TV as well. But the damage was done. Our critics chortled. In the midst of this, Aubrey was blamed, perhaps more than he should have been, for pushing the bloggers toward pompous corporate respectability. The fault was at least as much mine. But the solution wasn't simple, either.

Some bloggers may have rejoiced in our funky name, but the mainstream media used it to cut us out, even to make fun of us. Fox News producers wouldn't put Pajamas Media in their chyron (the crawl at the bottom of the screen). Did they think we were a porn company? I even heard that Matt Drudge, that well-known pillar of respectability himself, didn't like our unprofessional name and wouldn't link to us because of it. (Later this ostracism was rescinded.) Trying to strike a balance between online rebel and viable company was harder than I'd expected. I was beginning to see that being a businessman, something I had once disdained, could be as difficult as being an artist.

Another problem that arose at the inception of PJM was more personally disappointing. As indicated above, we had wanted the main portal to be a place where the Left and the Right could meet and discuss issues in a civil manner. But beyond that, it was our contention—here I may have been projecting—that there was a large number of hitherto unrepresented political hybrids out there, people like me whose views could be considered right-wing in some areas and left-wing in others. In my case, I supported the War in Iraq, but also was in favor of gay marriage. Many other permutations of various issues are obviously possible.

We confirmed this belief while ramping up to our debut by conducting a poll of voters via Princeton Research. Over forty percent claimed to be hybrids of diverse stripes. Michael Totten and Steven Den Beste, among other respected bloggers, underscored this view in their writings with specific theories about people's real political opinions—the ideological poles were not as popular as they appeared. We were a nation of hybrids.

The problem was, this complexity didn't translate easily into the real world of online discourse. When the portal was up, realizing that the word hybrid had come to be associated with cars, we ran a contest to name this new form of independent thinker. The winner was "free-ranger," but the contest itself didn't evince much interest. The majority of readers often seemed more interested in bashing their opponents, confronting the "moonbats" at the Daily Kos or the Huffington Post, just as the Kos Kids delighted in eviscerating the "wingnuts" at Pajamas Media. On all sides we had been brainwashed by our culture and the mainstream media into viewing politics as sports. Who was up and who was down was far more popular than thoughtful analysis. Economic forces increased this polarization. Money was to be made on the extremes. Hannity and Colmes were a hit for a reason. Al Franken and Ann Coulter hadn't become best-sellers on account of their judicious views.

While I was wrestling with this disappointment, Charles Johnson was growing uncomfortable with the corporate life. He never could stand going to meetings. A born loner, the former musician preferred to go off by himself to write his blog and play his music. As a particularly outspoken critic of Islamofascism, he was also rightly concerned for his personal security. After a while this became too difficult for all of us and Charles resigned as a company officer.

I was left to run things myself, but I didn't know nearly enough about how to do it. I was a vision guy, if I was anything, but the "vision thing," in Bush 41's words, can only take you so far. The business has to work. Furthermore, this vision which began as rebellion was rapidly becoming commonplace, as so often happened in this technological age in which Moore's Law appears to govern the media almost as much as it does microchips. Only microchips tended to get faster, smaller, and more efficient, while the media went spinning off in many directions, not all of them positive. The Internet had created a volcanic era of creative destruction in news and opinion distribution, but the eruptions were so constant they were almost impossible to harness.

Fortunately, Sandra Rozanski—a tried and true business school graduate—came aboard Pajamas Media, saving me from my worst instincts. She is now COO. But no one seemed to know what the new model would be, as newspapers contracted and laid off staff, even as those same mainstream media staffers had begun blogging themselves, sometimes not to particularly good effect. Blogging, after all, is ruthlessly meritocratic, a true free market of ideas and writing. On the web, a reader votes with his mouse whether he wants to continue with something or not, and that vote is recorded. No one knows who is reading what in a newspaper or magazine. Many journalists, some even quite well known but cosseted for decades by the reputation of their periodicals, found this new atmosphere a rude awakening. Not very many people were interested in what they were writing.

The more successful bloggers, meanwhile, were having trouble monetizing their popularity. Part of the reason for this was the reluctance of advertisers to spend much money on the Wild West of blogs, for fear of being associated with rudeness or bad language or, worse, a blogger who might criticize their product. But more importantly, a newfound caution had emerged among advertisers with the demise of print media. Suddenly they had the ability, via mouse clicks, to get real feedback on whether their advertisements were being read or, better yet, translated into sales. These click-through rates proved to be close to miniscule and were used by the advertisers to drive down the price of advertising even on websites with well-heeled and well-educated readers. Mass Internet advertising networks offered these advertisers hundreds of millions of page impressions for relatively tiny CPM (cost per thousand impressions) rates.

New media companies like Pajamas Media and The Huffington Post, aiming to create the "newspapers of the future," emerged in this treacherous business environment. It's not easy, but PJM, as we call increasingly call it, has had some notable editorial successes. Led by Omar Fadhil of Iraq the Model, our coverage of the first Iraqi election was more extensive and detailed than anything provided in the mainstream media. Our exclusive video of Iranian dissident Zahra Kamalfar and her family trapped for months in Moscow's Sheremetyevo Airport helped to convince Russian authorities to release the woman so she and her children could fly to freedom in Canada. We have also had the most thorough coverage in American media of the Paris trial of the French media critic Philippe Karsenty in the matter of the faked videos of the supposedly murdered Palestianian boy Mohammed Al-Dura on France 2. Exploding such instances of mainstream media prevarication is one of our specialties. We have had more than our share of failures as well.

Many people assume Pajamas Media is a successful institution because it has an increasing—often respected—presence on and offline. It also has a high demographic, its readership, as determined by a Nielsen survey, being above the *Wall Street Journal*'s in income and education. Yet our future remains precarious. In the midst of this struggle, however, I have been a lucky man, given a second life and a whole new education after my movie and fiction writing careers. PJM has brought me many new contacts and friendships I never would have dreamed of making.

Who knew that those nefarious neocons Michael Ledeen and Richard Perle were pussycat personalities and boon dinner companions? Their media myths and their realities couldn't have been more different. Perle is a gourmet cook and bon vivant with a house in Provence, hardly the "Prince of Darkness" of press reports. Ledeen, fluent in Italian, is a dog lover who listens to country music. He and his wife Barbara became two of my best friends. I've also had the privilege of introducing distinguished writers and journalists like Ron Rosenbaum, Victor Davis Hanson, Roger Kimball, and Claudia Rosett—not to mention my old actor friend from *Enemies*, Ron Silver—to blogging via PajamasXpress blogs.

And, of course, interviewing John McCain—in one of the Internet's first forays into high definition TV political interviews—on the night of his victory in the New Hampshire primary was an experience I won't forget. McCain has a reputation for a short temper, but he showed none of that when I met him. He exuded charm and confidence. I was also able to interview Rudy Giuliani that same day and, earlier, Fred Thompson, viewing presidential politics 2008-style from a more intimate angle than I ever would have expected. And now with the advent of Pajamas TV, we are expanding rapidly into the burgeoning arena of Internet television with the first high definition network online (PJTV).

My experiences at Pajamas Media have not always been fun, of course. As a screenwriter and novelist you get your quota of bad reviews and nasty insults, but they are nothing compared to the assaults you undergo on the Internet, which can be non-stop and are now written in indelible digital ink. (In the old days, bad notices faded away in the nether reaches of libraries; now they pop up perpetually in a three-second Google search.) You will find high in my Google ranking a man named Kenton Kelly, who blogs under the name of Dennis the Peasant and was briefly involved with the formation of Pajamas Media. Because we decided not to include him in the business, Kelly evidently considers me somewhere between Gilles de Rais and Attila and has gone on to tell the world as much with the devotion of a medieval scholiast, albeit an obscene one. Such, I have learned, is the nature of running a business in the digital age.

It should be obvious by now that I cannot predict the future of Pajamas Media or my role in it. It could be gone by the time you read this book, or purchased by Google, or still trudging along like many other start-ups. Yes, it keeps me up at nights, but my screenwriting career did, too. It's the nature of the things I choose to do. Much as I might yearn for a bit of peace and quiet, I wouldn't have it another way. If there's anything I fear more than insecurity, it's boredom.

9 FATHER TIMOTHY
AND MY THREE WIVES

Some of the most important figures of the Hollywood Left are not themselves entertainers or producers, but what are known in *Variety* as "non-pros." Through fame, charisma, money, or a combination, these "civilians" (another *Variety* term) come, for a time, to epitomize the Tinseltown zeitgeist. Among the better known of these is Stanley Sheinbaum, the retired economics professor and *Ramparts* editor who married Betty Warner, the Warner Brothers heiress. Sheinbaum cut his teeth on liberal fundraising for the defense of Daniel Ellsberg in the Pentagon Papers case (1971–1973), for whom he raised the then-princely sum of $900,000. He went on to be a national leader of the ACLU and the chairman of its wealthy and influential Southern California branch. These liberal bona fides, plus the Warner fortune, have made Sheinbaum one of the Kings of the Hollywood Left.

Parties at the Sheinbaum/Warner manse were and are grand affairs. Invitations are coveted more so than the usual Hollywood party's. The normal parties you read about in *Vogue* are attended out of the desire to see or be seen, or, most pathetically and almost always incorrectly, the dream that it will get you a job. With Sheinbaum, it's different. You never know who will turn up at events at his Brentwood home. Once it was a real king—the late King Hussein of Jordan. Another time it might be Prime Minister this or Chancellor that. Of course, there is more than a little bit of hypocrisy and inflated self-importance in all this. Not long after his visit from King Hussein, Sheinbaum went around the Clinton Administration and tried to be a personal peace emissary to Yasser Arafat. This hopeless and self-aggrandizing act of publicly appeasing the murderous kleptocrat placed him, temporarily at least, firmly in the category of Lenin's "useful idiots."

But the players on the more bohemian "charisma only" side of the Industry non-pro spectrum are at least as interesting and certainly more glamorous. They also may have a more enduring effect on Hollywood lifestyle and values. Probably the most prominent of those, until his death in 1996, was the guru of psychedelia himself, Timothy Leary. Sometimes it's hard, from the perspective of a new millennium, to remember what this man meant to my generation, but the former Harvard behavioral psychologist personified the Sixties as much as Bob Dylan, Jerry Garcia, Allen Ginsberg, or even John Lennon, especially when it came to the consciousness-expanding possibilities of drugs. The Swiss chemist Albert Hoffman may have brought LSD to the world, but it was Leary who popularized it.

I knew Timothy far better than I know Sheinbaum, whom I've only met a few times. When I first encountered Leary in the flesh, I was turned off because it was at one of those trendy parties filled with actors fawning over him. I was fascinated, too, because it was, well, one of those trendy parties filled with actors fawning over him. He was a living legend, after all.

Timothy must have been in his sixties then—it was the mid 1980s—but he looked great and none the worse for a whole lot of wear. He was tall and lean with a full head of thick white hair, firm pale skin, and those piercing blue eyes I recognized from a thousand love-in pictures. And, for all that had happened, nothing seemed remotely scary or druggie about him. If you put him in the proper attire, he could have been a parish priest from his family's native Ireland, and in some way he probably was.

The event was held at the small, surprisingly nondescript Laurel Canyon house he and his wife Barbara were renting—no ankhs or Tibetan pinwheels in evidence. I was married to Renee then and attended through her connection with Oliver Stone. Stone was already a friend of Timothy's. Of course, "friendship" here, among the Hollywood hipoisie, was as superficial as one would imagine—alliances formed for reasons far more important than mere personal affinity. That could come later, if at all.

Everyone at the party seemed quite chummy nonetheless. I lurked in a corner, watching. Leary and Hollywood—it was obviously a symbiotic relationship. Hollywood gave Timothy glamour and potentially money, which, I soon learned, he desperately needed. For his part, Timothy conferred a smattering of social relevance, intellectual panache, and pseudo-spiritual depth to a bunch of notoriously superficial thespians who needed some of that, at least for a time. Apart from Oliver Stone and Leary's own wife, I was probably the only one in the room who, because I was so deeply involved with the Left myself, knew Timothy's dark and politically complex history—for instance, that he'd reputedly ratted out his old comrades to the FBI to get out of the maximum security New York State prison where he'd been incarcerated on long-term narcotics charges.

A year or two later I attended an after-hours performance by Leary at a local comedy club. He wasn't the slightest bit funny, but who cared? The guru proclaimed the Los Angeles entertainment industry the epicenter of an ongoing world cultural revolution. Naturally, the audience lapped it up.

Still, I was dying to meet the guy, and had been ever since my sophomore year at Dartmouth in 1962, when my roommate Alan Coggeshall commuted to Cambridge to be one of his and Richard Alpert's first guinea pigs in their LSD experiments. Afraid that my mind would be blown permanently, I'd been too cowardly to go along. Even though Alan ended up committing suicide, I've always harbored regrets about not trying the drug with him. The degree to which LSD might have been involved in Alan's demise was never clear.

Not surprisingly, a lot of the conversation at the party revolved around drugs. I struggled to stay interested, but when the subject turned to computers, I perked up. Leary had an early, messianic interest in online community. He started holding forth about its possibilities. In response, the actors all looked the other way aimlessly. They could not have cared less. I, however, had been one of the first screenwriters to use a computer. So, as it happened, I'd already experimented with the fledgling Internet/Arpanet and was the only one there who knew what the hell the guru was talking about. We bonded.

Over the coming months, we continued our machine-inspired bonding, especially once Timothy realized that my overall "coolness quotient" was sufficiently up there due to my successful series of Moses

Wine mysteries. We would send pre-email messages to each other's terminals, consisting mostly of "Are you there?," "Yup, I'm here," etc., just as one may walk down the street this very day to the chatter of everyone on their cell phones, saying, "I'm walking up Sixth Avenue now, coming up to 14th and making a left. Where are you?" Timothy was my first cyber pal and I his, to my knowledge.

Cementing our relationship also was the curious serendipity that his wife, Barbara—a lanky, intense woman with a butch haircut who chain-smoked from a cigarette holder—and I were both graduates of Scarsdale High. She was also, on the surface at least, reassuringly bourgeois, the kind of woman who discussed clothing sales with Renee and where she got her hair done. So we did a fair amount of socializing with the Learys as they moved up in the world, to more luxurious (though still rented) digs in the Sheinbaum's very Brentwood. Barbara's exceptionally handsome and precocious eleven-year old son Zack—legally adopted by Timothy, who seemed to be a good father—went along with them.

Usually an event at the Learys' was a circus out of the hippie past, with characters like Wavy Gravy mingling with punk rockers, and studio execs and actors trolling for parts more intently than for any sex or drugs. Once, Renee and I arrived for an intimate dinner for eight. During dessert, Timothy casually asked if any of us had "done crack." Conversation came to a screeching halt. Sophisticated as this group might have been, crack meant underclass addicts and violent neighborhoods dangerous to white people like us. After a dramatic pause, Timothy smiled and allowed that *he* had. At a crack house in East Hollywood. He said it was "not what you expected" and "amazingly enlightening." He wanted to do it again—*right then*! Did any of us want to join him?

More silence ensued, followed by nervous coughs. Timothy looked disappointed (this may have been feigned). Then he fixed his gaze on me, saying, "Why don't you come, Roger? Moses Wine would, wouldn't he?"

I sat up straight. Did he expect me to know karate because my character did? I had been challenged before to live up to my adventurous detective hero, but normally it didn't involve a potential mugging in a latter-day opium den. Nevertheless, just to make up for wussing out on those Harvard LSD experiments, and after a sideways glance at Renee, who, wisely, had already demurred on the feeble grounds that she was "too tired," I assured her I'd be back early and said yes to Timothy. Within minutes, he, Barbara, and I were en route from Brentwood to East Hollywood—a thirty-minute trek even at midnight with little traffic. I was designated driver, a job I was pleased to have, mainly so that I could be in as much control as possible of our moment of exit.

The crack house was a decaying, six-story stucco affair in the badlands between Yucca Street and the Hollywood Freeway—in those days, junkie and hooker central. Timothy rang the bell. A rangy black kid in a t-shirt opened the door almost immediately. (He had been phoned). He looked about eighteen and held a baby in his arms. Other babies cried out in the background from other parts of the house, which reeked of a variety of odors ranging from frying hamburger to something suspiciously like vomit.

"Hey, Timothy, my man!" He gave Leary the Eighties equivalent of a high-five. I remember wondering for a second if he had any idea he was greeting the man who coined "Tune in, turn on, drop out!" I'm almost certain he didn't, and I doubt that he would have cared if he had. What he saw in front of him was just what he wanted—a tall white-haired middle-class geezer with cash.

We clomped up the stairs behind the young man, past those screaming babies and some mothers and grandmothers, to a room full of cushions on the fifth floor. A price of one hundred dollars apiece for a round of crack seemed to have been negotiated—by whom and at what I rate I didn't know or care to ask. The young man and his buddies, ever the conscientious service provider, had determined that Timothy and Barbara were a couple and that I was alone. I might need "company." I was asked if I wanted it, but declined.

Then we reclined on the cushions to wait. In short order, the crack pipes arrived and we toked up. Though I did this fairly gingerly, I was taking off for Alpha Centauri within a megasecond. I don't know if I would agree with Timothy that it was "amazingly enlightening," but it was sure one hell of a high.

And extraordinarily brief. It took you up to the ceiling, or I should say the stratosphere, and then back down to Earth in about two and a half minutes, at least it did for me. Then you were ready to do it all over again—a kind of rat-in-a-maze process, with us rats reaching for the lever again and again. I could see right away how so many people had become addicted. I could almost have been one of them myself, but I seem to have a genetic failsafe mechanism against over-indulgence in drugs or alcohol. My body always rebels before the second joint or the second (well, third) martini. In this case, the atmosphere also was turning me off. The sad desperation of that world—the crying children and their teenage, undoubtedly unwed, mothers. Not exactly conducive to flights of consciousness expansion. Or to the validation of any social values I felt then or now. Ten minutes after arriving, I was ready to leave.

Timothy felt differently. Before I had a chance to object, he and Barbara ordered a second round of pipes. Just then, a woman appeared. She was white, Southern, I gathered from her accent, and attractive in the blowsy manner of a Tennessee Williams character. She was also quite stoned—and looked to have been that way for some time. An addict.

She plunked herself down next to me, as if instructed to do so. Apparently the boys hadn't believed me when I said I wasn't interested in company. I tried to make this clear to the woman, but she, deliberately or not, disregarded what I was saying and began to rub my crotch, asking me to buy her a round and implying favors afterwards, which to me meant betraying my wife for a venereal disease. I desperately wanted to get out of there.

Timothy, already into his second crack pipe, began to regale us with tales of G. Gordon Liddy. Those were the days when Leary made most of his living through road show college campus debates with the former undercover operative and Watergate burglar—Liddy taking the "conservative" side and Leary the "liberal." I had always deprecated Liddy as a crypto-fascist idiot, but Timothy defended him, saying that his Hollywood friends just didn't understand him—that he was a lot smarter than we all thought he was. We were just prejudiced against a conservative, he said. I figured Timothy was just defending his meal ticket. In retrospect, Leary was quite correct. Liddy, a former editor of the *Fordham Law Review*, wrote the best-selling *Will*, and wound up with his own radio talk show in 170 markets. I don't know the guy, but his show is one of the more interesting of its type for the intelligence and wide-ranging background of its host.

But that night Timothy seemed particularly fed up with Hollywood, saying that his producer pals were all phonies because they never followed through on their myriad promises to hire him as an advisor on their movies and television shows. All they wanted was to say was that they knew Timothy Leary.

I could see that this hurt Timothy's feelings (he was naïve in some ways), but the Blanche DuBois beside me was suddenly deeply impressed. Unlike the owners of the establishment, she obviously knew *exactly* who Timothy was and what he represented. She struggled up on her stilettos, wobbled over, and plopped down next to him, whispering in his ear—loudly enough for all to hear—a menu including oral sex and other more exotic fare. I knew immediately that I had an ally in my desire to depart. "Let's go," I said to Barbara. She was on her feet in an instant, reaching down to help Timothy up.

Unfortunately, leaving wasn't going to be easy. The woman turned belligerent. She insisted we drive *her* home because she had lost her client. Which one of us that was supposed to be, I wasn't sure. Our hosts backed her up. I ended up dropping her off at her apartment in North Hollywood, after a pit stop so she could pee behind the bushes of a public park. Then I drove Timothy and Barbara back to Brentwood and returned to my house in Malibu. By that time it was nearly dawn and I had some "splainin" to do—"splainin" that I don't think Renee ever fully believed.

I saw Timothy less frequently after that night. I don't know why. Perhaps that one last adventure was enough. In any case, after Renee and I were divorced, I drifted away from that particular social set. Some years later, I heard he had contracted prostate cancer of a type said to be untreatable. I gave him a call, but he never returned it.

When I married Sheryl in 1994, my life intersected with his again, oddly. The year before we got together, Sheryl, also a screenwriter, had been visiting her friend Emma in Sag Harbor. Emma was a friend of Barbara Leary's, who by that point had separated from the sick Timothy and moved in with a rich Brazilian. Sheryl and Emma went to a party at the Brazilian's place in East Hampton, where Sheryl met Zack Leary (he'd taken his stepfather's name).

Zack, then nineteen, was even more handsome than when he was a young kid and had "movie star" looks with his stepfather's eyes, impossible as that sounds. He also was tremendously likeable. He was shuttling back and forth between his mother in the Hamptons and LA, where he tended to Timothy, who was surrounded by an array of herbalists and other quack healers. Zack developed a crush on Sheryl, who was ten years older than he. But Sheryl didn't find that out until *she* was back in Los Angeles and got a phone call from Emma in Sag Harbor. Barbara Leary wanted Sheryl's phone number for her son.

A short time later Zack took Sheryl for dinner at an expensive restaurant. He was charming, she told me, but liked to smoke dope a lot. Not for her.

A year or so later, shortly after Sheryl and I were married, we went to a party at Sheryl's friend Angela and her then-husband Gerry's house in the Hollywood Hills. Timothy, a friend of Angela's as well, was there, but he looked ghastly, on death's door, and stood awkwardly by himself in a corner behind the hors d'oeuvres table. The party was filled with movie stars—Gerry was a manager—who now seemed to be ignoring Timothy. The time had come for the Industry to move on to fresh gurus. Feeling sorry for him, I waited for the appropriate moment and walked up to him. *Remember me?* I asked, doing my best to smile. Timothy stared at me blankly.

Soon he was dying. A self-described "futurist," Timothy had always been interested in cryonic suspension—the experimental process by which the terminally ill are frozen until science has found a cure. We had discussed it on several occasions, and Timothy (a spokesman for two fledgling cryonics companies) had tried to sign me up, if not for the full-body experience, at least for the more popular head-only freezing—the theory being that it is our consciousness and not our body that we would want to reclaim in the utopian, disease-free future.

But Timothy apparently had had a falling out with the two companies, and by the time of his death he'd elected for cremation over cryonics. His ashes were now to be buried in space aboard a ship carrying the remains of twenty-four people, including *Star Trek*'s Gene Roddenberry. Apparently, if we are to believe a small independent movie that was made of his death, *Timothy Leary's Last Trip*, this never happened. Timothy is seen in the film indeed being decapitated, his head frozen for posterity. This was a fake, however. It was an obviously phony decapitation performed for an amateurish film, Oliver Stone having long since split the Timothy Leary scene.

The auteurs all turned out in force for Timothy's funeral. A true Hollywood affair, it was staged, appropriately enough, in a hangar at Santa Monica Airport. Barbara greeted Sheryl and me and the rest of us as if she'd never left Timothy. (She was actually his fourth wife.) Many of the familiar faces from the old days were there, the legends of hippie-dom and filmdom. Although several spoke, the two eulogists I remember best were Winona Ryder and Zack. Timothy had been Winona's godfather. A child of the Sixties, her father, Michael, had been Leary's archivist and ran a bookstore called Flashback Books. The actress delivered a simple but affecting speech, thanking Timothy for his inspiration to us all, and for tuning us in and turning us on. This was still several years before she was arrested for shoplifting at the Beverly Hills branch of Saks Fifth Avenue.

But the real hit of the star-studded event was Zack. Charming and mature, he was the anointed knight, carrying on his stepfather's tradition. He gave the longest and most riveting eulogy, assuring us all that our guru was transcendent and that he had indeed been cremated, his ashes safely rocketing into the firmament. Everyone went home, it seemed, in good spirits, as Timothy would have had it.

And that was the end, I thought, of my involvement with the Learys.

But it wasn't.

A couple of years later my first wife Dyanne called me to ask my opinion of a possible new tenant. Some time after our divorce in 1982, she had started to let my old office in the high tech house we had built in the mid-seventies. This concrete and glass bunker where I had written many of my first novels and screenplays was built on the garage level on the far side of the house. Isolated, with its own bathroom, it made a perfect rental. The possible new tenant was Zack. Barbara, who knew the house and was now living mostly in Brazil, had heard from somebody or other about the vacancy and arranged for the contact.

I found the coincidence amusing and recommended Zack to Dyanne as a tenant. Although my contact was intermittent at best, I told her I thought Zack was the most levelheaded and intelligent of the Learys. I couldn't have been more wrong. It wasn't long before I heard Dyanne was having numerous problems with the still young man, not the least of which were disputes about non-payment of rent. Meanwhile, Zack,

I learned, was in trouble with the law over some heroin allegedly found in his car. Was this an imitation of stepfather? I never associated the hard drug with Timothy, though—who knew—the son may have outstripped his famous stepfather in that regard. I didn't follow the ins and outs of it, but soon enough Dyanne was asking Zack to move out. She had long promised the room to a young woman artist who was a family friend and Zack—lost, frustrated and rather more devious than I had expected—was resisting. His mother too was stamping her foot long distance from South America and New York. It all came to a bad end with Zack finally moving on to ports never clear, at least to me.

This denouement left me rattled. What had they meant, all those years of freedom and experimentation? Just Timothy Leary's stepson disappearing into the Los Angeles night, another anonymous addict, if that's what he was? What was it all about, Alfie? Barbara, in this reading, was just a typical Boomer narcissist, a woman who left her son with a dying Timothy while she went off to seek a new life in Sao Paulo with a Brazilian plutocrat.

But then, as Jean Renoir has said, "Everybody has his reasons." Much as that famous quote may be a prescription for great filmmaking, I have always felt that it was also a license for bad behavior. Poor Zack Leary was the victim of an entire generation.

Of course, he isn't the only one, not by a long shot—just symbolic because of his stepfather. And, yes, there are some good Hollywood Left parents. I like to think I was one, but I don't know how I can, considering my two divorces, various affairs, sex, drugs, and rock and roll (well, not much rock and roll). Still my sons, Raphael and Jesse, turned out fine. Now in their thirties, they're terrific men, not the slightest bit addicted to anything, and living full and rich lives. But I ascribe this to blind luck and DNA. I have seen many other cases in this town that haven't worked out as well—and not just because of drugs but from myriad forms of dysfunction (depression, anorexia, etc.). I could fill the rest of this book with them. Being born into a world of stretch limousines ferrying mon-eyed guests to farm worker fundraisers fosters contempt for parental hypocrisy even in a stable home—and most aren't. The parents are not living anything close to the lives they espouse. Children see this immedi-ately. They always do. Where do their values come from, then—family or otherwise?

Hollywood people love to criticize the Religious Right. I was one of them, still am. I'm not particularly religious and organized religion embarrasses me, even my own. It seems like primitive superstition. But when it comes to raising children—which, if you're not Beethoven or Jonas Salk or Jean Renoir, can be the most significant thing you do in life— the Religious Right has a lot to teach Hollywood. Maybe more than a lot.

10 OJ CHANGED MY LIFE

That sounds like a headline from the *National Enquirer*, but it's true—partly, anyway.

When people ask me about my relative soft shoe to the political center after decades as a dedicated left-liberal, they usually say something like, "You're one of those 9/11 Democrats, aren't you? Like your buddy Ron Silver?" I mostly nod. It's hard to deny that 9/11 altered my view of things considerably. But what I almost always don't tell them is those views were already changing—because of the OJ Simpson trial. In a sense, weird as this may sound, the Juice prepped me for 9/11.

Now, with Simpson reappearing in Vegas like one of those childhood nightmares that won't go away—*The Mummy Returns*, as it were—memories of the trial and that time in Los Angeles are flooding back to me. It's also worth noting that just a few months ago, I was introduced at an event to one of the Simpson lawyers, Peter Neufeld. He seemed a pleasant, friendly guy, but I remembered how during the trial he and his partner Barry Scheck's actions especially disturbed me—of which more below. Memories were returning even then. (At that recent event, I asked Neufeld, perhaps a bit disingenuously, to write a Simpson Trial Retrospective for Pajamas Media. He declined.)

It's hard to believe how the OJ trial dominated our lives, particularly in Los Angeles, during those halcyon pre-9/11 days, now almost a decade and a half ago. It was as if a whole city stood still for the latest news of what Johnnie Cochran and his legal team were up to—whether the glove fit and you must acquit, what the latest dish on that allegedly racist (now celebrity) cop Mark Fuhrman might be, whether LA homicide detective Phillip Vannatter had completely bungled the investigation, or where Kato Kaelin cut his hair. And this went on for the better part of a year.

I'd had my own very glancing brushes with Simpson—I'd met him at parties and thought him, as did most people, to be jovial, handsome, and harmless—before that night of June 12, 1994, when Nicole Brown Simpson and Ronald Goldman were stabbed to death.

Besides doing my own writing, I was teaching screenwriting earlier that year at the American Film Institute. The students came to my house and I plied them with Cabernet to keep us all distracted. (There's not that much you can teach about screenwriting—either you can do it or you can't.) One of the students was OJ's personal assistant and, on my recommendation, worked on a screenplay to star the Juice. One of the things I could teach was how to use your connections, obviously a valuable lesson in Hollywood.

As a class exercise in creating a protagonist, I had the student tell the group what Simpson was like. Apparently, he was a non-stop womanizer (no surprise there) who liked sports and fast cars (again, not much of a surprise). He was self-centered (ditto). What evolved was a rather humdrum script about a retired NBA (not NFL—that was the clever fictional disguise) star who lived in Malibu, drove a Porsche, and solved crimes. I can't recall exactly what those crimes were—routine stuff, I think, like cocaine busts. But the script was clearly designed for Simpson, perfect for his limited range as an actor, even though his most recent films had bombed. Needless to say, nothing happened with the screenplay. A comeback, as it turned out, was not in the cards.

At the same time, I was about to get married. Sheryl and I were already living together on June 12, looking forward to our wedding day slightly more than a month off. Like most of the rest of the known universe, we watched the Bronco chase on television in stunned amazement, never having seen anything quite like it in history and assuming (correctly, as it turned out) that OJ was guilty. What innocent man would be behaving like that?

By then Sheryl had heard most of the stories about my involvement with the civil rights movement and later the Black Panthers, detailed in this book, not to mention my early brush with identity politics working with Richard Pryor. Still, it never crossed our minds at the outset that the black community would be such *staunch* defenders of Simpson. He lived, if anything, an upper-class white lifestyle, hanging out at swanky Brentwood parties in the company of well-tended California blondes; if not an "Oreo," he was the closest thing you could be to it after having spent your life in professional sports. (I never heard anything out of OJ's mouth similar to the racist diatribes recently credited to Isaiah Thomas.)

How wrong we were. By jury selection, Los Angeles was again a racially divided community. This time the roles were reversed—it was the African-American community whose behavior was racially motivated. All evidence being equal, it was hard to imagine the white population of Brentwood voting to acquit a white celebrity who had murdered his African-American wife and a bystander.

And that evidence...! As a crime writer who had spent years watching trials for professional reasons, I could not remember a single murder case where there was even remotely as much. DNA alone would convict Simpson a thousand times over.

We all know it didn't. Soon enough, Cochran was making a fool of the hapless Lance Ito and the befuddled Chris Darden. Marcia Clark, who was supposed to be such an ace prosecuting attorney, proved to be a paper tigress.

But worst of all for me were the aforementioned Barry Scheck and Peter Neufeld. These young lawyers had been doing God's work, having just a couple years previously founded The Innocence Project, which used newly-developed DNA evidence to free innocent people on death row. Now they were turning that on its head, exploiting their august reputations in the field, feeding false evidentiary distortions to a confused and eager jury, helping make this group of black women believe in "reasonable doubt" when Scheck and Neufeld knew bloody well the "reasonable doubt" they were selling was a trillion to one shot and that racism alone made the sale. What a shameful betrayal of their own good work. And for what? A moment in the sun? Of course they would defend themselves by saying that everyone is entitled to a fair trial with a vigorous defense. But how vigorous? And at what expense? I wonder how they feel now with OJ in custody, as of this writing, charged with multiple felonies.

And no one, as we all know, has since found even a remotely possible suspect in the Brown/Goldman murders other than OJ, not even someone "from the world of Faye Resnick," as Johnnie Cochran posited in a shameless act of dishonesty and character assassination.

But one thing you can say for Scheck and Neufeld—they weren't racially or ethnically motivated. Those two Jewish men had no trouble making sure the Jewish Goldman family would be tortured for life—or if this did bother them, they certainly did a good job of hiding it.

Sheryl and I and everyone else we knew in LA debated these things endlessly. We spent a lot of time personally on the OJ trail as well. We would drive by the Mezzaluna Restaurant on San Vincente, where Ron Goldman worked as a waiter, and retrace his steps to Nicole's nearby condo, trying to make our own evaluation of events. As it happened, the home of a producer friend of mine, Paul Witt, abutted OJ's manse on Rockingham, so I had a pretty good idea where that was and could trace the run from there to Nicole's as well.

Even the Ritz Carlton in Laguna Niguel, where Sheryl and I had our all-too-short honeymoon that July (I was on the committee doing pre-strike negotiations between the Writers Guild and the studios and had to return), figured in the trial. As it turned out, OJ had arranged for Nicole's father to own a Hertz franchise at that very hotel.

Not surprisingly, we had a great desire to attend the trial ourselves. But it was the hottest ticket in town, and we weren't high enough on the food chain. Early one morning, though, we decided to go downtown with our friends David Freeman and Judy Gingold to see the spectacle at the courthouse. A small city of satellite dishes and media trucks had been erected to accommodate the immense global interest in the trial and that alone would be worth braving LA traffic.

When we got there, however, all we found was a lottery for, as I recall, about a dozen remaining seats. It looked hopeless, but Judy won and we all got in. There we were in the small courtroom sitting only feet away from people who were then more famous than movie stars or even most rock musicians—Ito, Cochran, F. Lee Bailey, Robert Shapiro, Clark, Darden, and, of course, OJ himself. The witness on the stand that day was LAPD criminalist Andrea Mazzola, a poorly spoken woman whose testimony could not have helped the prosecution very much.

As she droned on, OJ, about ten feet away, turned around and smiled broadly at Sheryl. He practically *winked*. She didn't know how to react. We both agreed later on that he was flirting with her, and I felt a twinge of jealousy. Wearing an expensive suit and designer tie, the man had clearly not lost his looks. At that point in the trial, too, he was feeling confident of acquittal, and it showed. Eventually, the sociopath turned away and fixed his attention, at least superficially, on Mazzola.

I remember looking over at the jury. The women were sitting there stone-faced, probably trying to hide their boredom with peripheral testimony. This was the fourteenth week of the trial. I started to feel sad. What had happened to America that things had come to such a pass that a group of black women were about to free a rich black celebrity who had butchered his white wife and a friend of hers? This wasn't 1934 but 1994. We weren't in the world of Richard Wright—or were we?

I searched around for an explanation, and still do, for why the promise of the civil rights movement had never fully been realized. These women, largely from South Central Los Angeles and similar neighborhoods, lived lives light years from OJ's and his friends' and yet they still bent over backwards to defend this man who'd essentially deserted them. The psychological reasons (shame, rage at the "white bitch," and so on) were clear enough, but this stuff was as old as the American subconscious. Surely these women could rise above it. But they couldn't.

The obvious answer, the cliché, was that we hadn't done enough, not enough aid, not enough affirmative action. But sitting there that day, and in the weeks to come, I started to consider that the reverse was true. Well, not quite the reverse. We had not done too much, but we had done well enough. At the point of history America had reached, probably had already reached some years before, affirmative action had become an albatross around the neck of those who received it. Aid given to people— no matter who they are—when it is not earned carries with it a level of insult and denigration. It comes from on high to down low and carries with it an implicit message of lowness.

I began to think of Johnnie Cochran as condescending to the African-American community, as their enabler, treating them like children who would believe something as imbecilic as "If the glove doesn't fit, you must acquit." Cochran was in a way the racist in the way he dealt with his own people. He was certainly a racist in the way he dealt with white people.

I didn't say that out loud in those days, at least not very often, but I began to think it. It was the first chink in my very traditional liberal armor, the first time I thought outside a conventional wisdom that I had never questioned in my life. The groundwork was prepared for a larger questioning after 9/11. The OJ trial began it all.

Years later, after I had started blogging but before Pajamas Media came into existence, I was contacted via my blog email by a man who said he was a major campaign organizer and fundraiser for the Democratic Party. He invited me to lunch. I won't reveal who that man is here, because he has asked to remain anonymous and I have an acquaintance-ship with him that I wish to continue. But trust me when I say that he is responsible for many very successful campaigns for politicians whose names you would recognize.

At that first lunch he asked me whether I'd changed my views because of 9/11. I said yes, reflexively, thinking that he had done the same and not having digested, yet, the impact the OJ trial. To my surprise, he said that he was many years ahead of me. I asked him how that came to be. "Because of what the Democratic Party did to black people," he said, going on to talk about Maxine Waters, Jesse Jackson, et al., and how they profited when African-Americans maintained victim status. He sounded like Larry Elder or even, in his good moments, Barack Obama.

11 WHY THEY HATE THE NEOCONS

A few years ago, when I was first publicly called a neoconservative, I had only a vague notion of what it meant. Yes, I had heard they were former lefties, some Trotskyites or Trotskyists (another distinction that continues to confuse me), who had switched over to the conservative side and that they favored the promotion of democracy by militant means, when necessary. But that was about it.

At that point I tried reading a bit of the neocons' supposed founding father Leo Strauss, but found him heavy going. Maybe you had to have been there—the University of Chicago, circa 1952. In any case, I wasn't excited to be identified with them. If there was one thing I loathed being called, it was "conservative," neo-, paleo-, or any other kind. This was not my self-image from the time I bought my first copy of Miles Davis's *Birth of the Cool* somewhere around its release in February 1957. I was thirteen then and eager to try my first marijuana cigarette.

Still, I had been categorized. But it wasn't until quite recently when I read Joshua Muravchik's fine essay "The Past, Present, and Future of Neoconservatism" that, despite knowing several people regarded as leaders of the movement, I got a simple, clear picture of what neoconservatism was. According to Muravchik, it was divided into two schools: one, led by Irving Kristol, centering on a reexamination of the welfare state, and the other, led by Norman Podhoretz, focusing on winning the Cold War and now the War on Terror through democracy promotion.

My chief interest has always been in the latter and I find it ironic that the same high school me who was gobbling up *Birth of the Cool* was also a devoted reader of *Commentary*, the magazine Podhoretz then edited and where Muravchik's essay later appeared. *Commentary* was to me in those times just another part of my adolescent self-definition, like wearing a beret and turtleneck, listening to Mulligan and Monk, and going to beatnik poetry readings in the Village. I didn't know I was in the hands of the neocons. They just sounded smart and wrote well.

Those "Cool-School" days were a half decade before many things changed in our society with the advent of the civil rights and anti-Vietnam War movements, both of which I participated in heavily. So I am a typical product of my generation. I apologize for taking so long to get to my point about "Why They Hate the Neocons," but this is a Just So Story of a sort, as in "How the Neocons Got Their Trunk," so please be patient. This is where it begins to intersect.

As is well known, by the end of the Vietnam War, many of us came to the conclusion there was something seriously wrong with America. This generally entailed ignoring the obvious fact that there will be something wrong with all societies since they are composed of fallible (to put it mildly) humans. We were the big guys and we were therefore at the greatest fault. And one of the clearest areas of our villainy was that we supported or at least tolerated right-wing dictators like Pinochet, Somoza, and the Arab potentates. Although I didn't fully realize it then—I considered myself at that point aligned with the New Left—the neocons agreed with that. They pointed out, however, that our opposition to leftist dictators in China, the Soviet Union, and Cuba was justified. Their position against totalitarianism was consistent. Mine, and my friends', was not. We gave a pass to Fidel and company.

Perhaps it was that I got to visit the People's Republic of China quite early (1979) and later Cuba and the Soviet Union (twice) on cultural exchanges that I began to see those countries, as I have noted earlier, as gigantic jails. Still, I lived in a curious twilight zone where many in my generation found themselves, sympathizing, in principle, with the egalitarian socialist ideal while encouraging, even helping, writers and other dissidents to escape those societies. Hello, cognitive dissonance! It was all part of who we were, the way we were, if you will. Again, as I have noted, my trips behind the Iron Curtain were considered "groovy" in Hollywood. They gave me panache. We were light years beyond the blacklist.

And then something happened. Eastern Europe started breaking away from the communist world and the Soviet Union fell. Never mind that the reviled Reagan may have had some responsibility, everyone—or at least most everyone—rejoiced. It wasn't just a totalitarian system that was dissolving; socialism as an economic system lay in tatters. To call it "scientific" was laughable. The Left was left with little to do, little to organize around. (Bill Clinton, recognizing this, essentially deserted his own side by walking back on welfare issues). Of course, there were gay rights to be resolved, but the rapidity with which most of those rights were being achieved was astonishing. It has been less than forty years since the Stonewall Riots to the general societal equality of gays in nearly every context but marriage. The Left was the victim of its own deserved success in the social justice area when...

9/11 happened.

The U.S. suddenly had a common Islamofascist enemy. Something had to be done. But there were no philosophical underpinnings for the confrontation, no groundwork. This was a whole new world. Only one group had been consistently warning of this situation all along—the neoconservatives. They had a solution in democracy promotion, the elimination of Middle Eastern despots. They would be our gurus.

Soon enough, it appeared the neocons had taken over the government and Bush and Cheney were acting at their behest. As Muravchik points out, since neocon policies were then the clearest common sense response, it's unlikely Bush and Cheney needed this prompting, but nevertheless the popular media view is that they were in the neocons' grip.

So in those slow motion moments when the 767s crashed into the World Trade Center, everything switched around. The cool guys in school were no longer the cool guys. One clique—the alliance of lefties, hippies-cum-yuppies, the liberal media, and showbiz types—moved out, and some admittedly semi-stodgy ex-Scoop Jackson policy wonks moved in.

Idealism had been stolen from the Left. (In truth, as I indicated, they didn't have much remaining, but that probably made it all the worse.) This constituted an insult to a lot of people's self-images. The neocons were to be hated because they had stolen that idealism. In a sense, they had stolen those same people's youths. For a very short period, Abbie Hoffman had morphed into Paul Wolfowitz. The neocons were to be envied then. And no doubt they were.

This was indeed a short period, because such a deep insult cannot easily be tolerated. The depth of the hatred it evinced is clear in the unimaginative lyrics of the Rolling Stones' "Sweet Neo Con": "You call yourself a Christian / I think that you're a hypocrite / You say you are a patriot / I think that you're a crock of shit." Forget that Mick and Keith chose to overlook (or were unaware) that neocons are normally assumed to be Jewish; their principle point seems to be that all this democratic idealism is bogus. The war was really about corporate greed and we know it. The song contains the usual casual references to Halliburton and Brown & Root, as if it were written on the john while skimming *Newsweek* and swigging a bottle of Guinness.

But reducing the Iraq War to mere profiteering is unfair reductionism. I wonder if, at other moments, the Stones really believe what they wrote. Have the Street Fighting Men turned into pacifists who believe that all wars, including World War II, are wrong, since all wars have profiteers? Whether the particular companies they enumerate are even profiteering is open to question. Some say they are having financial difficulties from participating. Moreover, you don't need to read Victor Davis Hanson's or Michael Yon's latest report from Iraq to know that most of our soldiers and even many of our leaders were and are engaged in what is to them an idealistic enterprise. Whether it was the right idealistic enterprise is subject to debate, but the basic impulse of these people, our soldiers and those leaders, should not be. It is the converse of calling someone a traitor for criticizing policy.

So why the anger? Why the willed distortion? Jagger and Richards were of course far from the only ones. You could find this kind of hostile schoolboy name-calling in a Frank Rich column in the *New York Times* and a Keith Olbermann screed on MSNBC, to name just two of thousands. The attacks began even before the war in Afghanistan, but by the time we were in Iraq, it was a cacophony. Somebody's ox had been gored. Idealism is the good guy's province. When your idealism has been stolen, you are no longer the good guy. You are the bad member of the family. No one wants to be that—a loss of love is involved. But what do you do?

One thing you do is to try desperately to retrieve the moral high ground. Two approaches to this have been employed: running down your competition (in this case saying that his project has failed and trying to ensure that it does) and building up your own alternative. This, in part, accounts for the rise of the global warming issue as a religion. A societal consensus had long ago been reached on environmental and energy concerns. Conservation and alternative energy promotion were considered to be good things, but now allegiance to them crosses the bounds of science into the devotional sphere. You are on one team or you are on the other team. You are either with us or against us.

In all this we've come to a terrible pass, and I think many of us feel it. I know I do. We have come to a point where, because the psychological-emotional-personal stakes are so elevated, we routinely deny the other ones. On both sides of the ideological divide, where idealism is so deeply fought over, we refuse to acknowledge our opponents' humanity—that, no matter which side they're on, they can come from a place of wanting the best for people. I know that I've suffered from that and, I am ashamed to say, have responded in kind on occasion, sometimes also unfairly. Where we go from here in this battle, I don't know. But have some sympathy for the neocons. They may be under attack currently, but if we do actually win in Iraq, as now seems likely, for them there will be hell to pay.

12 THE NEW BLACKLIST

People often ask me whether my political change hurt my Hollywood career—whether I was and am the object of a new reverse blacklisting that discriminates against those who, as I did, publicly supported and continue to support the Iraq War or, worse yet, voted for George W. Bush in 2004.

In all honesty, I don't know. Maybe I wouldn't have had much of a career, anyway. The insider joke about the old Hollywood Ten from the *original* blacklist was that none of them was any good at that point and that the glamour of being blacklisted kept them alive and in the public eye. Of course, that was an unfair accusation, not only to Dalton Trumbo, but also to Ring Lardner Jr., who came back from the blacklist to write *The Cincinnati Kid* and the original *MASH*. Albert Maltz, who wrote the WGA-Award-winning *Broken Arrow* under a pseudonym and later *Two Mules for Sister Sara* under his own name, was no slouch either.

In my case, it's likely I lost *some* work, but I would have to have a clone to be sure what would have happened to me in the last half-decade or so had I continued my life as it was. I'd like to think that my public stand against Islamofascism cost me a half-dozen Academy Awards, but that would be blowing my own horn in the extreme. Hollywood careers are fragile at best, especially for writers. And mine wasn't at its height at the beginning of the millennium. I was a decade past my Academy Award nomination and I was getting on in years for the business in general. Writers deep in their fifties are not the most sought-after commodities in the film industry for a number of reasons, including a notorious inability to tolerate story meetings with twenty-five-year-old studio executives fresh out of Wharton who haven't seen any movies predating *Spider-Man 2* and think *Chinatown* is a downtown neighborhood with overpriced lofts. It's also true that older writers, as experienced and skilled as they may be, may not *be* the perfect people to write films for the Industry's most coveted demographic—the sixteen-year-old male—even though that audience is now much more heavily engaged playing computer games, which, I am told, are considerably more interesting than today's movies. That wouldn't be difficult.

The Hollywood screenwriter is in a classic trap. By the time he has fully learned his craft, he is ready for the thresher. (When I was in college, my doctor father told me one of his patients—obviously a movie exec—had asked him in a baffled tone, when informed by my father that his son wanted to be a screenwriter, "Why not a producer?" I rolled my eyes at the time at what I thought was outright philistinism. Now I realize it was just practical advice.)

But beyond *my* place in *them*, the movies were losing *their* allure for me. The film business—engulfed by conglomerates from Paris to Tokyo— was becoming increasingly corporate and boring, nowhere near the fun I remember it having been. At the same time, cinema itself was no longer central to the culture the way it had been in the Sixties, Seventies, and even most of the Eighties, when everybody—including a sunglassed dog in a legendary cartoon, sitting at the desk of his CAA agent—said he wanted to direct. It was part of the zeitgeist. Who could forget the buzz when films like *Breathless, La Dolce Vita, Apocalypse Now, Bonnie and Clyde,* and *Lawrence of Arabia* were coming out? There was nothing like that now, at least not for me. Society had moved on. We lived in a time when technology was king, Steve Jobs more important than Francis Ford Coppola or Federico Fellini. Marshall McLuhan had been proven right—the medium really *was* the message, the iPhone more important than the films played on it. Meanwhile, on television, I was finding reality shows like the Discovery Channel's *Deadliest Catch* more interesting than any fictional story.

In other words, regarding the movies and me—the feeling was mutual, and it was no longer love.

So I haven't lost sleep worrying about whether or not I was blacklisted. Still, I am sure this new form of the blacklist exists, but not nearly to the formalized extent of the original list of the Forties and Fifties with its Red Channels and dramatic hearings in front of the House Un-American Activities Committee, featuring "friendly" and "unfriendly" witnesses. Times are different and the system functions in a very different manner.

Now it operates through an almost invisible thought control caused by a post-Orwellian "liberal" conformity so pervasive that a formal blacklist is unnecessary, and, indeed, would work against itself.

In some ways, this new, less overt list is worse, because there is nothing concrete to rebel against, no hearings, no committees, no protest groups pro or con, no secret databases. There don't need to be. There is no there there, in Gertrude Stein's immortal words—only the grey haze of this mindless received liberalism, the world as last week's *New York Times* editorials, half-digested and regurgitated, never questioned, going forth forever with little perceived chance of reform, as if it were the permanent religious text of some strange new orthodoxy.

You see this new faith in practice at the average Hollywood story meeting. These are ritualized events and have been for the decades that I have participated in them. You wait an inordinately long time for your appointment, often longer than at a doctor's office, but with nowhere near the legitimate excuse on the part of the executive keeping you waiting. They are definitely *not* in surgery. The intention is merely to confirm your *lower* place in the pecking order. (I have personal knowledge of an instance when John Huston and Jack Nicholson were kept cooling their heels in a tiny room by the now-forgotten head of ABC Motion Pictures for nearly two hours—I assume he didn't realize they'd come to pitch him *Prizzi's Honor*. Or maybe he did and this was a form of envy or vengeance.)

Once inside the executive's office, the pecking order of talent and management thus confirmed, it's instantly waved off in a burst of small talk and a call for the requisite mineral water—originally Perrier, now something more exotic like an obscure Welsh brand in a blue bottle whose unpronounceable name you can barely remember. But the small talk is what's important. It usually revolves around the freeway traffic (a perpetual subject), the Lakers (depending on the year), and, over the last half-decade or more, a ritualized Bush bash. (What will they do without him?) *Fucking Bush did this or that... Did you hear the stupid thing Chimpy the Idiot said?* You didn't even have to hear Bush referred to specifically—the word "idiot" sufficed. You *knew*. The subtext was that we were all together, part of the secret society, the world of those who know as opposed to those who don't.

If you didn't agree with this particular *Weltanschauung*, if you dissented from its orthodoxy just a tiny bit, you had but three choices: One, you could argue, in which case you would be almost certain to be dismissed as a fool, a warmonger, or a right-wing nut (all three, probably) and therefore have had little or no chance at the writing or directing job that brought you there. Two, you could shut up and ignore it (stay in the closet), in which case you felt like a coward and experienced (as I have) a dose of nausea straight out of Sartre. Three, you could stop going to the meetings altogether—you could, in effect, blacklist yourself.

I don't know the size of that self-selected blacklist, but I suspect it's substantial, though certainly not as large as the number of those in the closet. People have to make a living, after all, as in the days of the old blacklist. Only there are no "fronts," as in the Woody Allen movie of the same name. No one has come forward to ask me to ghost write an anti-war movie, a remake of *The Battle of Algiers*, say, set in Sadr City, although, with my radical past, I suspect I could do a better job of writing left-wing movies than Hollywood has lately, judging by the box office receipts.

There are many reasons for the failure of those movies, but chief among them was *not* what the right-wing blogs said—that they were out of touch with the public. That may have been true to some degree (issue movies, taking at the very minimum nine or ten months to make, usually considerably longer, are almost always somewhat late to market as far as public opinion is concerned). It's that they were *fake*. In other words, these films weren't really believed in by their *creators*, in any deep sense. They are a cinema of "as if," and those who see it sense it unconsciously.

This is the opposite of a movie like the classic of classics *Casablanca*, a film that triumphs with its audiences for being heartfelt. Hollywood's new anti-war flicks are essentially posturing. They are cinema made by people who think they are *supposed* to be anti-war, but don't really feel *anything*. No wonder the audiences didn't respond. (This wasn't true of a few of the Vietnam War-era films that had more genuine passion, just as the demonstrations against that war were vastly more impassioned and well-attended.) Sometimes, as in the case of Brian De Palma's *Redacted*, these films seem to have been made to rescue a failing career by demonstrating the "correct" political views. This may have been unconscious, or barely conscious, on the part of the filmmaker, but true nevertheless—cynical as that accusation may sound.

For evidence you need go no further than the subject of De Palma's movie—the rape and murder of an Iraqi woman by U.S. troops. This choice of theme is intended to convey a message against the Iraq War, but horrid events of this nature have happened in *all* wars on *all* sides, including World War II, when GIs are known to have raped and murdered German women. Thus De Palma's point is irrelevant and propagandistic, unless he wants to say we should never fight a war, which, of course, he doesn't. (Nazis, in Hollywood's received wisdom, are still bad.) He wanted to say we shouldn't fight *Bush's* war, the *Republicans'* war.

In this particular case, the Army punished the servicemen involved, casting further doubt on the director's premise. It's unlikely, however, that De Palma cares. He is, after all, a member of the club—or fighting to get back into it—and lives in the world of the pervasive haze I have described above. To him, thinking that way is natural, like breathing. It is a kind of "going with the flow."

Meanwhile, those flailing against this flow have a tough time. Some of this is obviously political. The system has excommunicated them. But some of it is due to this uncomfortable truth: For the most part, Republicans are lousy filmmakers. There are exceptions, but not many. Clint Eastwood, who keeps his politics out of his films for the most part, is the exception that proves the proverbial rule. If you don't believe me, compare the quality of the presentations at conservative film festivals like the Liberty and American Renaissance Festivals with Toronto, Sundance, and Jackson Hole (to pick only North American festivals). The level of work at the two conservative festivals borders on embarrassing. You're relieved when there is something even professionally competent. In recent years, incredible energy at these festivals has been squandered on an obsessive drive to counter the films of Michael Moore, as if focusing on this narcissistic liar-filmmaker would make his documentaries go away, rather than just publicize them further.

Other standbys of these festivals have been worthy but pedestrian documentaries on Islamofascism, which employ cinematic techniques reminiscent of a Fifties grammar school short on tooth decay. (In fairness, Al Gore's global warming documentary, for which he won an Academy Award, is equally ham-handed.)

The standard explanation for this Republican creative deficit is that conservatives in general have not wanted to be artists—particularly theatrical and film artists or storytellers—and therefore have not had much practice. I think it's more complex than that; psychological issues are also at play. Some of it has to do with the conservative personality and its innate risk aversion. Artists, particularly literary or dramatic artists, storytellers, are typically asked to live, or are portrayed as living, on the edge. They are asked to explore things for the rest of us that we don't do (or admit we do), to report back, as it were. The cliché goes that there is nothing so old as the avant-garde, but still artists are to some degree the avant-garde of whatever time. Most conservatives, however, live like, well, conservatives. They are the rearguard. This is never clearer than in the context of film, with its young audience and emphasis on the new.

A portion of the conservative view in our society is faith-based, and that doesn't help with the creation of compelling characters, either. People are seen as inherently good and evil, a worldview that, while theologically defensible, can severely limit dramatic possibilities. Human motivation is simplified; it becomes boring and predictable, not artistically exciting. Irony, the most useful of dramatic devices, is often conspicuously and pitiably absent.

Another exception that proves the rule here is the immense popular success of Mel Gibson's *The Passion of the Christ*, a cinematic event that more closely resembles a medieval Passion play than a film as we generally conceive it. The movie does not seek to persuade or create a "willing suspension of disbelief," to seduce you into the story, or even to convert you to Christianity, but instead *recreates* New Testament events in a manner regarded by the filmmaker as faithful. As with Passion plays of yore, believers were greatly moved by this. Those of other religions, atheists or agnostics (like me), regarded it as a well-made curiosity. Some, however, were repelled by the violence. Gibson's delusional anti-Semitism also makes it harder to accept.

The more important—and hopeful for the future—exception to the general lack of conservative film creativity are Trey Parker and Matt Stone, the authors of the *South Park* television series and films. They have been able to throw off the mantle of propriety, that enemy of art, and eviscerate left- and right-wing targets. They have shown that conservatives can be just as outrageous as the Terry Southern and Stanley Kubrick of *Dr. Strangelove*. Who can forget their image of Satan and Saddam Hussein locked in a highly sexual romantic embrace?

Parker and Stone's fearless satire is all the more potent for appearing in an era of pervasive liberalism. Further, for Parker and Stone's willingness to take on subjects across the ideological spectrum, their popularity speaks for a new generation that is to some extent post-ideological or least tired of restrictive conventional definitions. Count me as one old guy who applauds that.

13 THE RISE OF THE "MINI-ME"

So what we have in today's motion picture industry is an uneasy mix of a small number of as yet relatively incompetent conservative artists (with exceptions) with a majority of disingenuous but sometimes talented liberal ones. The liberals are living in their own version of the past—an illusory Sixties—which is comfortable and highly remunerative for them. Growth and change are not applauded. Despite the recent losses on anti-war movies and the evident audience dissatisfaction with liberal preaching, staying with the conventional wisdom *is*.

What is the reason for this? It's important to remember about Hollywood lives that, when successful, they are rewarding almost beyond comprehension. You become immensely rich and famous as an adult for living out the dress-up shows you did in your parents' living room as a six year old. What could be better than that, what more charmed life possible? This is true even though it regularly generates that split personality known as the "limousine liberal" or "Cadillac communist," the movie mogul inveighing against global warming from a private yacht in Tahiti the size of a destroyer.

If it were that simple, however, if this were *only* about hypocrisy—that storied homage that vice pays to virtue—we could just shrug it off as another humdrum wrinkle in our culture. It is, of course, more complicated, because the effect on the world is immense. American popular culture still predominates. The Hollywood liberal does not want to change his or her views for deeper reasons than preserving those multiple estates with a Prius in every garage. Serious issues of self-image and personality integration are involved. That adult who got to live out the wildest dreams of the six year old knows just how lucky he or she is compared to the rest of humanity, how tenuous that mega-success. Hollywood life is not secure even for the most famous. The powerful have had to claw their way to the top in a brutally competitive dog-eat-dog environment that has been well dramatized in such film classics as *All About Eve* and *Sunset Boulevard*. (Some of the best Hollywood films are about Hollywood. Write what you know.) Those who achieve in this atmosphere are quite often those who have learned to mistreat and step on others with impunity to succeed in the movie industry. Many are execrable in the way they treat associates, staff, and families in their private and business lives. Self-loathing lurks just below the surface. Also the fear of failure—of being "found out."

No wonder so many Hollywood personalities develop an alternate persona, almost a "Mini-Me" out of the *Austin Powers* movies, that is an extreme liberal wind-up Good Guy (or Girl) who parades as publicly as possible his unbound altruism and devotion to the poor and downtrodden. (A prime example is Sean Penn, who battered his wife, going off to save Katrina victims.) Then, once that Mini-Me is paraded and gets his applause and acknowledgment from the masses, he can be put away in his closet again. This Hollywood personality can resume his or her normal life, raping and pillaging all those who come in the way of success. It's a form of split personality or, more exactly, "splitting," in the language of the Chicago School of psychoanalysis, contradictory behaviors separated off from each other so that the cognitive dissonance is not so readily apparent to the holder of the disparate thoughts.

I first observed this phenomenon years ago—although it was too early to use the "Mini-Me" analogy to describe it—when I found myself surprised at how cruelly some of my more liberal, even radical, friends treated those working for them. It wasn't always the case—some were kind and decent—but it was too frequent to ignore. In fact, the exploitation of subordinates has long bordered on standard operating procedure in Hollywood. It was and is a town where assistants are routinely treated like coolies. No one seems to be able to drop her own clothes at the dry cleaners or pick up a pack of Diet Coke at the convenience store by himself. Status is obtained not only by avoiding such menial tasks, but also often by humiliating the assistant responsible for them.

I found that this disconnect between the public and private person becomes more pronounced the more successful he or she becomes. Ironically, the accepted wisdom of the liberal group I used to pal around with was that conservatives were "bad people," that there was something inherently wrong or greedy about them. Since these Brentwood liberals were some of the richest people I knew, I now think of this as a kind of projection and much of Hollywood liberalism itself to be *based* on projection—on the idea that the other must be greedy and selfish when, whether consciously or not, it is the liberal himself who is greedy and selfish. The accusations are a distracting charade, a flimflam job on the self and others, to preserve an opulent lifestyle by avoiding embarrassment and seeking inoculation from criticism. That former Senator John Edwards built a 28,000-square-foot house while railing against the iniquities of the "two Americas" during the last presidential campaign is an almost comic version of this. With his blow-dried hair, he would fit in perfectly in Hollywood, but as more of a plastic television series star than a feature player.

We are moving now into a time, however, when the presence of these "Mini-Me's" is more irritating to the public than it was, less well-received. It's even approaching the level of a national joke. But don't look for it to stop. For a certain kind of Hollywood narcissist, the "Mini-Me" is a necessary outlet. He cannot be denied. The answer to the problem of Hollywood for those of a more conservative or centrist bent is to go make movies of their own. Of course, to do so means finding financing and distribution. Today's technologies are making that simpler. Cameras and editing equipment cost a pittance. Distribution is at hand for the price of a URL. All that's left is the creativity. Unfortunately, that's the difficult part.

14 EXTENDED FAMILY VALUES AND *THE GODFATHER*

I am reaching the conclusion of this book shortly before becoming a grandfather. Somewhere around August 1, 2008, my son Raphael Simon will have twin girls. But not in the conventional fashion. Raphael lives in Los Angeles with his lover Phillip De Leon. The birth mother of their child lives in Ohio. The gestating twins come from Raphael's sperm and yet another woman's egg.

I am very excited by the coming event, but admit to mixed feelings. These have nothing to do with Rafi and Phillip being gay and having children. That is more than fine with me. Having children is the greatest of human experiences and I am sure they will be excellent parents. No, this is about me. I can no longer kid myself about being "Forever Young." Like many boomers, I have trouble adjusting to the reality of growing old. It's not for nothing that I wanted to write the screenplay *Freddie Faust*. And that was long before I knew I would be a grandfather.

Now I make bad defensive jokes to Rafi about buying a corncob pipe and rehearsing avuncular stories about the good old days of Aquarius when Yoko Ono was young and yippies danced around the maypole in Central Park, but I know I will adjust to the situation quickly the moment I see the twin girls. My daughter Madeleine, who is ten, cannot contain her excitement. She will be an aunt, just as her considerably older adult brothers Jesse and Raphael are her uncles (they call themselves "bruncles").

Our blended family may seem odd, yet I suspect it is not all that untypical. Through a combination of Enlightenment tolerance and basic longevity, the modern family is morphing into a heterogeneous racial, ethnic, and sexual cocktail. That too is more than fine with me, as well as are many of the outgrowths of these developments like gay marriage, which I support and see as a natural extension of the civil rights movement. (My attitude toward marriage is pathetically simple: I decide who I marry. You decide who you marry.)

I know I break with many on the Right on this issue, just as I break with many on the Left on what I believe to be more important: For the preservation of the Enlightenment and what allows us to have these crazy blended families, and all the freedom and benefits that go with it and other aspects of our lives, the battle against Islamofascism is the paramount issue of our time and trumps all. On this I have some conflict with Raphael who, being gay, sees gay rights as paramount. All politics is indeed local. When I point out that Islamism is the world's greatest enemy of gay and women's rights, and is growing in adherents, especially in Europe, he understands this view, but is reluctant to follow through to its logical conclusions. This is the kind of debate being carried on in families throughout America. I am lucky that in mine it doesn't break out into fisticuffs or even (very many) screaming arguments.

From my angle, part of the reason for this relative peacefulness and acceptance is love and part is self-image. The aspect of me that is still liberal does not want to be *seen* as intolerant of anybody—sometimes to the extent that I am being dishonest with myself. This jumped to the fore when Rafi came out to me as gay back in 1988. I was in New York for a book signing and he came down from Yale, where he was a student, to have dinner with me. We were walking down Broadway from the bookstore to the Café Luxembourg when he told me. My first thought was: *Hey, be cool. You're a liberal. This is perfectly okay.* Inside the restaurant I was all smiling bonhomie, asking my son which of the waiters he fancied. But when I got home that night I called my ex-wife and threw up.

Of course, I felt ashamed of myself for having difficulty with this revelation and told myself that I had to adjust quickly. That wasn't hard because I have always regarded homosexuality as biologically determined and the idea that people's sexual preferences could be adjusted via psychotherapy or faith to be laughably out of contact with reality. What was really going on that night was probably anxiety about how this would affect me—whether I'd be branded a bad parent for having a gay son—an absurd, self-centered way of looking at things. I got over it fast. Within a short time, Raphael and I were writing a thriller screenplay together about the relationship of a father running for office and his gay son. The premise was Rafi's idea.

Raphael is now a successful writer of novels for the ten-to-thirteen market. (In the family tradition, he recently had the same disappointing experience as his father of being nominated for an Edgar Award from the Mystery Writers of America and losing.) His brother Jesse—once an after-midnight graffiti tagger on the streets of LA with a group called the KGB (Kidz Gone Bad)—has grown up to be a professional artist represented by one of the most respected galleries in the city. A lifetime surfer, he refashions discarded surfboards into elegant wall-mounted sculptures resembling the paintings of Joseph Albers.

Still, I have been far from immune to the common family disruptions of the post-9/11 era. Although I have excellent relationships with my sisters Wendy and Martha, Martha occasionally looks askance at my political migration. (Hey, she's a *San Francisco* attorney.) My wife's mother Anita isn't bothered by this change, but Sheryl's brother Stuart also has trouble with it. Yet, ironically, it is my wife who saved my sanity during this period, making the same migration, step for step, as I did, although not revealing it as publicly. Without her, I'm not certain I could have held myself together through the process.

But such a dilemma was the furthest thing from my mind when I met screenwriter Sheryl Longin in a friend's kitchen at his fiftieth birthday party, which was a few months after mine. She was attractive, petite, and vivacious—just my type. My only thought at the time was, was she too young for me? Or, more precisely, would she think I was too old for *her*? Sheryl seems to have interpreted my apprehension as disdain, because the next day she told her writing partner Andy Fleming that she met that writer Roger Simon at a party and that I was inexplicably horrible to her. At that same moment, Sheryl was playing back messages on her answering machine—including one from me, asking her out. Fleming laughed and said that she *had* to go out with me just to find out why I'd behaved the way I had. I'm grateful to him.

We were married five months later and immediately found ourselves, as the Chinese curse goes, "living in interesting times." From the early Nineties onward we have been in an extraordinary epoch, although we didn't quite realize it at first. Sheryl and I were married July 17, 1994, about a year and a half after the first World Trade Center bombing of

February 26, 1993. Although somewhat abortive and largely ignored, this event marked the beginning of the assault on Western civilization by adherents of radical Islam.

In the midst of this, Sheryl was marrying a man twenty years older, someone she regarded as a "child of the Sixties" with all the inherent experience of that supposedly revolutionary period. But looking back, the Sixties and Seventies were a time of remarkable naïveté. (One of the fascinating aspects of what are called the Sixties is how close the days of flower power and Aquarius were to the Holocaust. 1968, now over forty years ago, was a scant twenty-three years from the liberation of Auschwitz.) My experiences then were but play-acting compared to what was before us. By September 11, 2001, Francis Fukuyama's 1989 proclamation of the "end of history" had transformed into a cruel joke.

Although the OJ trial began to change my life and worldview, September 11 altered it beyond recognition. I no longer identified as a liberal or as a traditional member of the Democratic Party. First I would describe myself as a 9/11 Democrat, later as unaffiliated with any party at all. For the first time in my life I voted for a Republican when I punched the ticket for Arnold Schwarzenegger in the California recall election of October 7, 2003. The only times I can recall not voting for a Democrat prior to that were once or twice for a Peace and Freedom Party candidate at the height of the Vietnam War—and then on a whim for a down-ballot position like county comptroller. Other than that, I'd been a loyal Democrat since I accompanied my father into a voting booth at the age of nine, helping him pull the lever Gladly for Adlai like ninety percent or whatever of all the Jews in New York.

When I finally came to vote for Arnold, I didn't know if I could actually cross the threshold. But Sheryl and I did it together. (She'd been a Clinton organizer in Little Rock in 1992 and felt trepidations at least equal to mine.) By the time we got to the presidential election of 2004, we were old pros at apostasy. Even so, that was an odd experience, voting for Bush in our polling place high in the Hollywood Hills where Democrats outnumber Republicans by roughly the ratio Chinese outnumber Armenians in Beijing. I felt like I was traveling incognito behind enemy lines and voted for several Democrats as well just to make sure I didn't get caught, or to reassure myself that I hadn't gone completely crazy.

Sometimes I feared I was dragging Sheryl into a *folie à deux*, but I realized that she was far too intelligent for that, too much her own person. It was she who often saved me from too ardently embracing the Right out of my indignation towards the reactionary Left, reminding me that my social values were still distinctly liberal.

We were both doubly reminded of this when we returned to the movie business to write a film arising out of the War on Terror. The opportunity was exciting to both of us, not just because it was a chance to get back into serious filmmaking after a hiatus of several years. I had been acutely aware that the entertainment industry had been making one atrocious and biased anti-war film after another, when my friend Michael Ledeen approached me for a group interested in producing a fictional film about Iran. I immediately asked Sheryl to collaborate since she's such a good writer and because I was apprehensive about being able to write the script myself while doing justice to my day job running Pajamas Media. She'd be able to do more research than I.

But both of us were troubled by something. The principal producers of this Iran film were to be ex-Senator Rick Santorum and Steve McEveety, Mel Gibson's lineman for *The Passion of the Christ*. As social liberals and passionate believers in the separation of church and state, neither Sheryl nor I were enamored of Santorum. His remarks about homosexuals and his role in shutting down Congress during the Terri Schiavo affair were quite disturbing to us. We would have to swallow a lot to work with him on this movie. Nevertheless, he had been an outspoken opponent of the mullahs. And the presence of our good friend and renowned advocate of Iranian freedom Michael Ledeen reassured us. The chance to make a statement against the Islamic Republic was too great to pass up because we disagreed with the social views of one senator. I urged Sheryl that we should do it and she reluctantly agreed.

The first meeting with Santorum at a hotel in Santa Monica was satisfactory. He is a tall, handsome fellow with the practiced charm of a politician. And he had a dramatic opening sequence—the movie would begin in the early Eighties when the Iranians under the leadership of Ayatollah Khomeini sent ten-year old boys across Iraqi lines as mine sweepers. It would be *Saving Private Ryan* with children. Our heroes would be survivors of this horror in which the kids were motivated by a desire to bring forth the Mahdi, the "hidden imam" of Shia Islam to whom Ahmadinejad and his supporters continue to owe their allegiance.

Santorum had other notions about the story only a few of which made sense to anyone who had written screenplays. Indeed, it was clear that he'd never read a script or even had much familiarity with the vernacular of film. He did not recognize our references.

But reluctance overcome, Sheryl and I were now eager and ambitiously set out to write a *Godfather*-style epic of the Iranian Revolution, tracing a family with members on various sides of the struggle from 1979 to the present. We tried to base as much as possible on verifiable fact. We went to Washington where, through Ledeen's offices, we were able to interview several of the courageous student activists who rebelled against the mullahs in the late Nineties. Manoucher Mohammedi, one of their leaders whose face looked like a cubist painting from having been repeatedly beaten in Tehran's notorious Evin Prison, particularly inspired us. The extraordinary bravery of his true story could be the emotional heart of our movie. We made a fictional Manoucher the central character of our drama, which ended with his confronting his younger brother, who'd become an officer in the mullahs' Revolutionary Guard, about to perform an act of terror in the United States.

We wrote quickly because the producers wanted to be in production in time for a release that would influence the electorate in the 2008 presidential election. It was a tall order, especially since we didn't have a director. McEveety, the only movie professional among the producers, was understandably nervous. But Sheryl and I were able to finish a draft in the allotted ten weeks, delivering it to McEveety, who was on the way to Pennsylvania to meet with Santorum. Evidently, much of the financing for the film was to come from the former Senator's wealthy supporters. After reading the script, McEveety called me, clearly relieved. It worked for him. He could now represent it to the investors. Ledeen also liked the script.

Then the other shoe dropped. Santorum didn't get it. None of the characters made sense to him. Where was the religion? Of course, there was plenty of religion in the screenplay, more than in any Hollywood film about Shia Islam by a fair amount, but it wasn't enough for the ex-Senator. To him everything and everyone was motivated by religion, almost exclusively. The characters had to be praying every five minutes and either were good moderate Muslims or religious fanatics. Mixed motives did not appear to exist and secular Iranians, like many of the student leaders, were of little or no interest to him. Maybe he didn't even believe they *could* be secular.

The modern Tehran visible to all on YouTube was news to him. It was as if he wanted us to write a medieval Passion play set in the Islamic world, a one-note melodrama among the devout. Sheryl and I didn't know what to do. We didn't speak the same language as Santorum. (Incidentally, I'd worked with a senator on a movie before, but it was nothing like this. I was hired to adapt William Cohen's *Murder in the Senate*, when Cohen was Maine Senator. Cohen was actually fun to work with and had a good basic story sense from writing thrillers, as well as some understanding of character motivation. He was also obsessed with Hollywood, taking calls immediately from Tri-Star studio chief Mike Medavoy—the executive in charge of our project—during our meetings in his Senate office, while waving off what seemed to me important Congressional business.)

Not surprisingly, the Iran movie ended badly. My last memory of the project is driving up Interstate 5 to Seattle in the summer of 2007, listening on my cell phone to Rick Santorum endlessly tell me his script notes in one of the more bizarre imaginable parodies of a Hollywood story meeting. (McEveety had completely vanished by this time.) Very few of these notes made even remote sense, but Santorum's not so hidden implication was that Sheryl and I had to do his version or else. It made me yearn for the likes of Harvey Weinstein or Michael Eisner. They may have been bullies, but at least they were bullies who'd made films.

I was frankly relieved that I didn't have to continue to justify to my gay son working with a Senator who had once appeared to equate homosexuality with incest. His defenders say this was strictly a legal definition, but whatever it was, my sense of the man was that his rigid religiosity made it difficult for him to see others whole, not a good prescription for the creation of art. But these are the times in which we live. In the terms of *The Godfather*, the enemy of my enemy is my friend. Or perhaps just as significantly, keep your friends close and your enemies closer. In any case, my own extended family values could only be stretched so far.

15 SATORI IN THE MODERN AGE OF CONSERVATIVE LIBERALS

I have often said that I'm uncomfortable being called a conservative—it's so square—but these days I almost always find myself getting along more with conservatives on political issues—except for social ones, as you can tell. Even there, I understand their position on abortion, even if I can't agree with it. And I recognize that many religious conservatives, as I indicated in my chapter on Timothy Leary, have more authentic family values than many liberals. So sometimes I feel as if my entire personality has been altered, that I had some kind of brain transplant turning me into a dyspeptic character out of a 1950s John Cheever novel, doomed to die of martini poisoning on a New Canaan porch.

But one day I had a blinding moment of low-rent *satori* and saw that all is not lost. (I can't remember where and when this was. I could make it up and say something dramatic like the Zen garden at Daitoku-ji in Kyoto, but why bother?) Just as sixty is the new fifty, fifty is the new forty, and so forth, *liberal is the new conservative.* There is nothing more conservative, more conventional and square, these days than a liberal—or "progressive," if you prefer that desecration of the English language. You don't even have to be as much of a *South Park* fan as I am to realize it—though I thank the creators of *South Park* for helping me accept myself and to see the truth: to be liberal is no longer liberal, and I am free.

And if you look all around you, you can see this. Who has a more orthodox, more rigid vision of life—today's liberals or conservatives? Well, again, let's except religious conservatives from this, because they tend to be less flexible, but economic conservatives and libertarians have remarkably divergent views and tend to tolerate the opinions of others. Sometimes they even *listen* to them. They even seem to be interested in their ideas. (Again, perhaps we should leave off Ron Paul acolytes, who seem about as tolerant of divergent views as Branch Davidians.)

The vast numbers of liberals I know are quite different. They almost never discuss ideas. They have a received value system, a litany of unquestioned beliefs resembling a religion. Of course, some of them are wonks, meaning they discuss the *implementation* of the ideas, but not the underlying concepts. Liberalism, their version of it, anyway, is a *donnée*. On further reflection—far, in this case, from satori and thus more suspect—that *donnée*, that version of liberalism, is meaningless because the real liberalism was accepted by Western society hundreds of years ago. Thus the current bourgeois and reified version becomes riddled with contradictions, as in attacking conservatives for being vigilant against Islamofascism, when Islamofascism is the world's most virulent enemy of women's rights and homosexual rights, justifiably two of the most accepted liberal shibboleths.

I have seen this played out in my personal life many times. Liberal friends do not want to discuss politics with me. At first that was mutual, because I was often afraid of alienating them. But as I came out of my shell, I saw fear in them. Very often they evinced little knowledge of subject matter, particularly about Islam. They had read little or nothing on the most controversial issue of our time. It was almost a willed ignorance, like the child from the Passover Haggadah that "wits not to know." Otherwise, of course, they would have to take some kind of action and that action was fraught with peril—alienation of friendship, loss of work and, worst of all, dissolution of personality. I can assure them that none of those things are so bad (he says mordantly).

Does this mean I am now a conservative? No. I am and always will remain the same old Groucho Marxist who would never join a club that would have me as a member. Having left the liberal orthodoxy, don't expect me to join another one. I now have fear of orthodoxies the way some have fear of crowds. Don't come near me with your orthodox ideologies or I will make the sign of the cross and ward you off like a vampire.

Okay, I overstate. Ideologies are fascinating, brilliant, and have a place—as long as they don't make you blind. But too often, they do. The minute you think ideologically you give up at least part of your ability to observe reality in the moment and to react logically. Is this devotion to the moment another Zen influence? Perhaps. I don't understand Zen very well, but I had my brush with it, as I mentioned earlier, during my divorce from Dyanne. It was the period of my life during which I felt the most depressed. A fifteen-year marriage was ending. I was being separated from my children. I worried whether another woman would find me attractive, whether I would be able to work effectively. All the familiar litanies of divorce. I sought refuge, as many do, in a psychotherapist's office. I came from a New York Jewish family, steeped in the tradition of Freudian psychoanalysis, but something prompted me to choose another road. I picked a man named Ed Wortz, who had been an engineer for the astronauts at one point—had designed underwear for them, of all things—and had then become a gestalt therapist with an interest in Zen.

At first I worried that this choice was "too California," not sufficiently rigorous to mend the deep emotional turmoil that was rending my soul. But, reluctantly and skeptically, instead of engaging in the endless talking cure, I sat down in the lotus position on a cushion in Ed's office with electrodes strapped to my head for biofeedback. It was scientifically enforced meditation. I would listen to my mind go in and out of the alpha wave, bouncing over to gamma the moment I had the hint of an anxious or depressing thought, or sometimes, apparently, for no reason at all. It was as if my unconscious was tracking my anxiety *before* it came to the surface. Gradually I trained myself to observe this process and, on rare occasions, to arrest it, not an easy task.

That was over twenty-five years ago and I don't know if it changed my life, but it may have to a small degree. Zen sitting can be an extraordinarily useful but difficult to maintain discipline. At its best, it positions you at the intersection of thought and emotion and allows you to reconsider your actions. Ed Wortz compared this to a diver poised on a board, slowing his plunge into the water by seeing as many aspects of his dive as possible.

This examination of process has some relationship to political evolution, the subject of this narrative. Politics for most of us is a highly emotional experience. We may think we arrive at our views dispassionately, but we are prey to a bevy of conscious and unconscious forces. I have certainly had mine. I remember being brought to my feet by a Rudy Giuliani speech at the Republican Convention of 2004 and by a Bobby Kennedy speech in the barrio of East Los Angeles two days before he was assassinated. Were they saying the same things? Unlikely. But actually I can't remember with any precision *what* they were saying—and that may be the point. As the playwright Hugo von Hofmansthal once put it, "Politics is magic. He who knows how to summon the forces from the deep, him will they follow."

I am suspicious of following that magic myself now—whatever person or ideology is summoning up those forces from the deep. Like Ed Wortz's diver, I try to stop myself before taking the plunge—or at least slow down the process. What I am left with is a collection of ideas with which I have dabbled throughout my life, never fully discarding any of them, even though some are completely contradictory of others. I regard Marxism, Freudianism, libertarianism, *laissez-faire* capitalism, Zen Buddhism, Quaker pacifism, neoconservatism, neoliberalism, that whole galaxy of isms, as arrows in a quiver to be drawn at will, depending on the adversary or the necessities of the situation.

That may sound dangerously close to yet another ism—cultural relativism—but I assure you it is not. I *do* think there is almost always a good and evil, a right and wrong—although often you have to look closely—and the relativist view of the world is at best lazy and at worst a stalking horse for fascism. Those arrows in my quiver are no more than an arsenal for helping me find that elusive truth. And perhaps for taking action. Sometimes one is not enough. Sometimes I don't need or want any of them.

Still, this does not really address my question at the outset of this book. Am I the same or am I a very different man from the young civil rights worker in South Carolina 1966? I could cop out and say you decide, but I'm sure, in your own way, you already have. And no one is exactly the same, obviously, after forty years. Yet I don't think I'm radically different. Some people have told me I am a "neoconservative," some a "classical liberal." If the latter means someone who embraces the Enlightenment in its basic values of freedom, then that is what I am and always have been, despite the fact that on any given day I could disagree with many of its precepts and even more of its adherents. But please don't call me one. You know, of all things, I despise labels.

INDEX

Ono, Yoko, 179
Operation Abolition, 17
Oppenheimer, J. Robert, 17
Opsahl, Myrna, 43
Ordinary People, 99
Ortega, Daniel, 116
Orwell, George, *Animal Farm*, 46
Osmond family, 49

Pajamas Media (PJM), 50, 84, 89,
    135–141, 155, 159, 183
Parallax View, The, 36
Parker, Trey, 172–173
Passion of the Christ, The, 172, 183
Paul, Ron, 188
PBS, 96
Peace and Freedom Party, 182
Peery, Nelson, 10–11
Penn, Sean, 176
Pentagon papers, 143
Perelman, S. J., *The Road to Miltown*,
    20
Perle, Richard, 140
Pfeiffer, Michelle, 88
Phillips, Michelle, 38
Pinochet, Augusto, 162
Pinter, Harold, 90
Pipes, Daniel, 135
Plame, Valerie, 137
Platoon, 74
Podhoretz, John, 28
Podhoretz, Norman, 28, 161
Pollack, Sydney, 80
Pollack, Tom, 31
Pons, Lili, 20
Powerline, 133
Premiere Magazine, 87
Pressman, Ed, 8–9
Previn, André, 94
Previn, Soon-Yi, 94
Prime of Miss Jean Brodie, The, 56
Princeton University, 16
Prizzi's Honor, 169

Protocols of the Elders of Zion, 114
Proust, Marcel, 101, 135
Pryor, Rain, 61
Pryor, Richard, 51–52, 58, 60–68, 84,
    156
Pryor, Richard, Jr., 61
Puente, Tito, 78
Putin, Vladimir, 107, 114

Quakers, 19, 190

Raisin in the Sun, A, 13–14
Ramparts, 143
Rather, Dan, 134–135
Reagan, Ronald, 118–119, 162
Redacted, 170–171
Redford, Robert, 98–99, 122
Reds, 38, 85
Reed, John, *Ten Days that Shook the
    World*, 36, 38
Rendell, Ruth, 84
Renoir, Jean, 85, 152–153
Resnick, Faye, 157
Revolutionary, The, 8, 80
Reynolds, Glenn, 132, 134–135
Rich, Frank, 164
Richard, Pierre, 122
Richards, Keith, 164
Richbourg, Lance, 31
Rinzler, Alan, 7, 25, 33–34
Rocha, Glauber, 8
Roddenberry, Gene, 150
Rolling Stone, 25–26, 32
Rolling Stones, The, 163–164
Rosenbaum, Ron, 140
Rosenberg, Mark, 54–57, 69–70
Rosenthal, Jack, 97
Rosett, Claudia, 141
Ross, Artie, 80–81
Roth, Joe, 87
Roth, Philip, 57, 109
Rozanski, Sandra, 139
Rubin, Jerry, 41, 59